ohn, Fischindustrie

et 1888.

05.   Emden, den   23. März   192 8.

kmann,   Hopsten   bei Beesten

Th. Hahn Wwe., G. m. b. H., Emden.

ahlungen sind nur an uns nach Emden zu leisten.

Rechnung und Gefahr per   Bahn

ringe   R⫞   60.–

nnerhalb 30 Tagen!

ei uns nicht eingegangen sein,
mit einverstanden sind, wenn
nziehungskosten erheben.

23/ͥ 28

August Jasper & Sohn
Emder Heringe
Emden a. d. Nordsee

18 - HARENG $(0^m20$ à $0^m30)$

SVERIGE 170

ÅLDERSBESTÄMNING AV SILL / TILLVÄXTRINGAR PÅ FJÄLL

TOM HULTGREN   ZLATKO JAKUŠ sc

ÖREBRO 02.11.82 ★ ★ AF

INSTITUT DES PÊCHES

PEACOCK

A Morning Catch of Herring.

HERRING

A LOVE STORY

DANIEL ROZENSZTROCH AND CATHIE FIDLER

SUZANNE SLESIN PUBLISHER
FREDERICO FARINA CREATIVE DIRECTOR

POINTED LEAF PRESS, LLC.

CHICOR

PAUL

LE HARENG

FÊTE DU HARENG

SUR LES QUAIS
24 et 25 novembre 2012

Réalisation : BD / ville de Fécamp - imp. Banse - septembre 2012

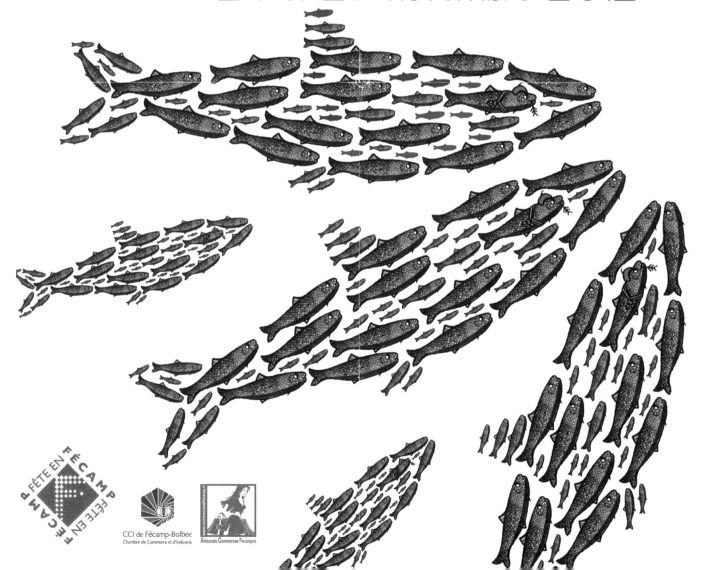

FÊTE EN FÉCAMP
FÊTE EN FÉCAMP

CCI de Fécamp-Bolbec
Chambre de Commerce et d'Industrie

Artisanats Commerces Fécampois

CONTENTS

I. IN THE BEGINNING

How on earth did we let ourselves get caught up in the nets of this herring adventure? Daniel and I have a little joke about that: "Just so we'd never let anything fishy come between us!"

You see, this is not just a book about a fish—the herring—but the illustrated story of a long friendship, a friendship cluttered with collections; for Daniel's the collector and I'm the friend who's forever nagging him about his obsession, just as his mother would have done: "Do you *really* need all this old junk?" Or else: "Wherever are you going to put it all?"

Long before our project took shape, Daniel had already baffled all his friends by accumulating, first, a mass of wire objects, then all kinds of coat hangers, and then, to cap it all, brushes! And every single time, this had led to something amazing—a book, an exhibition. We must admit, he's an original, and his collections are different.

You'll already have understood that Daniel is an inveterate collector, even a compulsive one. And that can be contagious, which is how I got myself embroiled in a wild-goose chase for images to illustrate our topic. But above all, both he and I came to realize that what brings us together is a most unusual collection: Shared memories. It's worth pointing out that these memories go back long before we were born and concern all that's deepest in our histories, in our shared culture and its symbols.

People are like that—they have symbols sticking to their souls.

The fish symbolizes abundant life, and our ancestors the Hebrews already recognized this in the *Book of Jonah*, even before the conversion of those poor fishermen through a "miraculous draught of fishes." So it was that the first Christians drew the primitive form of a fish in the sand, or on a pebble, in order to be able to recognize one another. It was a sort of secret code that enabled them to tell friend from Roman foe.

For the Khmers, the fish, symbolizing water, plumbed subterranean depths measureless to man. So it was sacred, just as it was for the ancient Egyptians, the Phoenicians, and the Mesopotamians. The Phoenicians ate plenty of fish, so much so that their descendants, the boastful men of Marseille, have a joke about a sardine that grew so big it blocked the mouth of the ancient port of Massalia.

For the *Indios* of Central America, the fish was a symbol of the corn god and so, of nourishment, even if they didn't feed salmon with any strange flour back then. In China, it's a good luck symbol, although it's surely luckier for the stork depicted by its side than for the fish that ended up as the stork's dinner. According to the Hindu tradition, the current cosmic cycle is that of the Fish – but let's not drown in those details. In the world of Norse mythology, magical beings manifested as fish: the god Loki

OPPOSITE This charming Dutch postcard, illustrating the place of fishing in the life of children in The Netherlands, could also allude to the childhood love story between the two authors of this book. OVERLEAF A 1910 postcard came with a very explicit message in French that can be translated as: "Happy 1st of April [April Fool's Day]. My card is serious." Herring fisheries located in the English port of Great Yarmouth had already been mentioned in documents that dated back to the 11th century.

REX ET NOSTRA JURA

GT YARMOUTH

Only a line

arrived - quite fresh

captured the dwarf Andvari, who turned into a pike, and that's part of the saga that inspired Germanic mythology, all the way down to the composer Richard Wagner.

We know that the fish is divine and its name is often invoked, sometimes in vain. Only what kind of fish? I've already mentioned the Marseille sardine, and I could add that every group of human beings has its own fish: the millers' wives of Normandy with their beloved *sole meunière*; in their Metro and their buses, Parisians are packed like sardines; the French say of some women "she's as flat as a flounder"; old harlots are called *morues*, or salt cod, and their pimps *maquereaux*, or mackerel; plain women are known as old fishfaces; of those who are forever wriggling and giggling, one says "she's like an eel; she never keeps still"; and of quiet ones, "she's as dumb as a carp."

If your guest is from the south of France, you'd better serve him a redfish or red mullets, not tench (doctor fish). If he's an Englishman, serve him cod, fried in batter and wrapped in newspaper, with a packet of the "chips" that Americans call French fries. Just mention dried cod to a Portuguese, and his eyes will light up like those of a fried whiting. The same for someone from Nice, except that he'll call it *stockfish* and eat it in a fabulous *estocaficada*, quite unaware that the main item in the dish comes straight from Scandinavia. Just like the herring.

By way of introduction, we've taken you almost around the world, without a safety net.

And yet, so far, I've not so much as mentioned a fish belonging to the *Clupeidae* family; to be more specific, a fish of the species *Clupea harengus,* better known as the herring, the king of the Baltic and, above all, the king of the Jewish dining table in all the countries of Central Europe. And it is the herring – fresh, smoked, and filleted – that is among the things that have brought Daniel and me together, over a period of decades. The very same herring that our forebears—who all came from about the same part of the world—ate for breakfast, lunch, and dinner, because they were so abundant, and consequently, so cheap.

This is where our family histories diverge a bit, for Daniel's ancestors in Prussia were not only tobacco and herring merchants, but coopers, makers of barrels. But not the kind used for transporting vodka (that's my Polish kinsmen by marriage—the Daumans—whose barrels did indeed hold vodka...). No, Daniel's people turned out those lovely little kegs made of light-colored wood in which herrings were packed before they reached their inland destination, where they were devoured by my ancestors. The French have a proverb that says "barrels will always smell of herring." That's another way of saying that we can't get away from our origins: We remain steeped in their smell, and "what's bred in the (fish) bones comes out in the flesh."

That adage brings me to another tale that brought us together—a tale of embarrassment, not to say shame. Over to you, now, Daniel:

"When I was little, I suffered from terrible bronchitis every winter. The doctor suggested to my mother that she should take me to breathe good North Sea air in the summer. So for several summers in a row off we went together for vacations at Scheveningen, an elegant seaside resort in Holland. I won't mention

OPPOSITE On the back of this card is an indication of the Dutch city of Scheveningen, with the notation "Everyday dress."

RIGHT As in other Dutch towns, every year Volendam celebrates the arrival of the new herrings, which are eaten in a very special fashion: Traditional costumes are worn, and it's a holiday, as can be seen from the many flags blowing in the wind—hence the name *Vlaggetsjesdag*, or "little flag day."

OVERLEAF Happy customers enjoy themselves at a herring stall in Amsterdam, on the Haarlem Lock. The card, which dates to 1954, boasts the merits of Holland in winter. Yet it's in the spring that herrings are at their best!

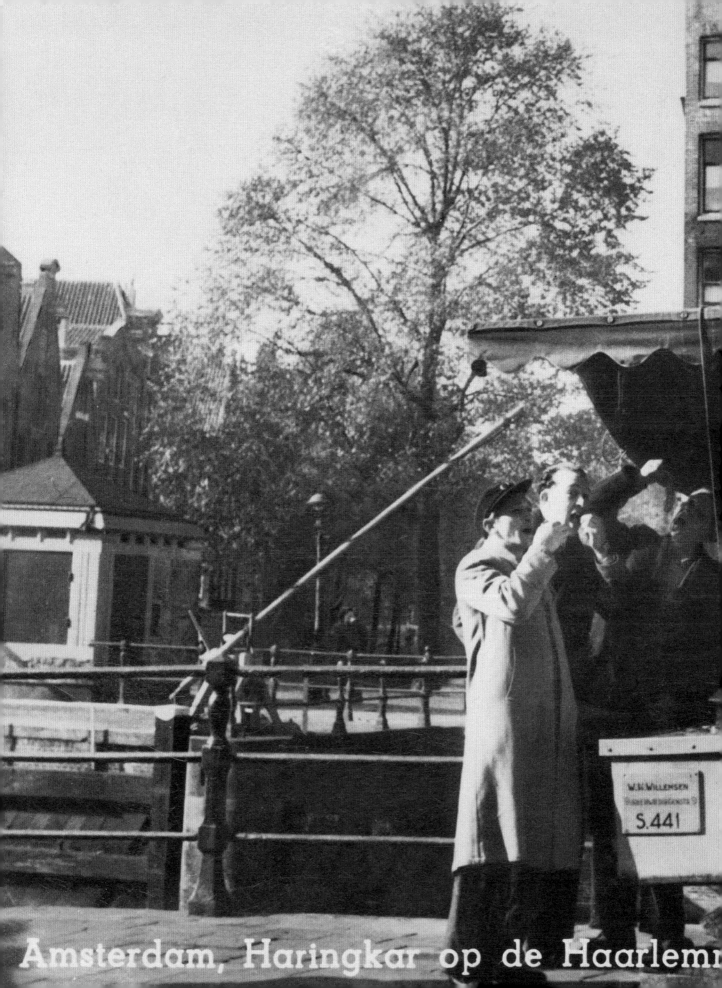

Amsterdam, Haringkar op de Haarlemr

all the details of those vacations in a lovely house not far from the beach—because the memory that has stuck with me is that of our return to Paris by train. I can still see my mother, loaded up with luggage, all sorts of suitcases and bags, but above all with two or three of those little kegs of herrings in brine. She'd handle them as though they contained caviar, or dynamite, laying them oh-so-carefully in the overhead nets—yes, nets—that they had in those days, above the hard benches, for hats, umbrellas, and small bags. Those kegs were well wedged in up there, yet I just couldn't keep my eyes off them—not because I cared about their contents, but out of shame. I was ashamed because the whole compartment smelled of them. I was ashamed of this business of transporting fish. Maybe I was subconsciously ashamed of the way the other passengers looked at us. So I'm not sure I was all that happy about those herrings appearing on my plate once we got home. Now, I could kill myself for having behaved that way! Oh, I'd sell my soul for one of those little kegs. I can still see them—made of very light-colored wood, with metal hoops… And, oh, the taste of those herrings… I still keep looking for them."

The thing that embarrassed *me* was rather more ordinary. It was to do with not being like everyone else. Yes, we ate herrings at home—and what Parisian hasn't eaten them marinated in oil and served with potatoes? Only, I lived in the South, where they're not all herring people by a long shot. What's more, my mother served them with sour cream, garnished with fine-sliced apples and big, fat dill pickles. Worst of all, she'd serve them to my uncle for breakfast! If I'd dared tell my classmates, I can't help thinking that would have forced me, if not them, to accept that I was different. But no, I couldn't do that. I took good care never to mention the existence of those dishes they didn't serve at school meals. And I really didn't know whether I liked them or hated them. I just ate them, that's all there is to it, without asking myself questions about their cultural content. Yet I should have, what with my mother's litany dinned into me day in, day out: "Your grandfather ate herrings every day. It was herrings in the morning, with a glass of tea, and a glass of tea with herrings in the evening, just to make a nice change." Enough to put one off herrings for life. There must be plenty of people who share that tale, if I'm to believe cultural anthropologist and cookbook author Claudia Roden, who quotes the English chronicler Chaim Bermant: "On Sunday one had a pickled herring, on Monday and Tuesday soused herring, on Wednesday baked herring, on Thursday herring fried in oatmeal, and Friday, herring in sour cream."

In the 1920s, a Jew would eat a herring a day…. Which of the two should we pity more?

In fact, the carp.

No, it's just not possible, before consecrating so many pages to the herring, to avoid the bitter memory of the freshwater carp, the other emblematic fish of Ashkenazi Jewish cuisine, which, before it was stuffed —or made into fishcakes, all the while keeping its name, *gefilte fish*—was borne home religiously from the market and plunked in the family bathtub. The reason for this baptism: to get it to cough up and sweat out all the filthy, indigestible matter it contained, as the carp's natural habitat is in muddy ponds. A few days later, the slimy beast was knocked out (with a rolling pin) by the lady of the house, both

OPPOSITE A poster advertising the Dutch seaside resort of Scheveningen, near the industrial port of The Hague, is typical of the graphic style of the 1920s. Written in English, it was aimed at the refined, cosmopolitan clientele that summered in the town.

chef and part-time executioner, before being cooked, with the (sickly sweet) result we all know. Let's not spell out Daniel's reactions, as a child, to this bloody domestic assassination. After that, it's hardly surprising he should have been fond of herring, as that fish's sad fate had been decided a long way from the bathroom.

The highly knowledgeable publisher of this book also has one of those unforgettable memories. Her Lithuanian mother liked to eat in the restaurant of the fancy Ritz Hotel in London. Now, don't let us forget that Britain came through World War II as much because of kippers as of Winston Churchill. Churchill stuffed the Britons' heads with his injunctions, while kippers (smoked herrings) filled their stomachs. Unfortunately, this dish came to be associated with hard times, so that it ended up being somewhat looked down upon in better days. But this lady's tastes had not changed and she stayed faithful to the herrings she had always loved. So, the minute she sat down for lunch at the Ritz, she asked for kippers, only to be told in most disdainful tones: "Madam, we only serve *those* for breakfast." It seems the chef had to break his rule that day. Some requests will not give way to British conventions. All in all, with a dish of herrings, we're swallowing as much culture as fish: When we eat them we are nostalgic for a bygone world, and trying desperately to catch in the net of memory all that's been handed down to us, without our even being aware of it.

So it was that one day it dawned on Daniel and me that, while herrings are part and parcel of our precious personal history, that history is also universal. Now we could reveal it—and, thanks to Daniel's splendid collection, we could even unveil it: all those beautifully decorated dishes in which we'd traditionally lay our famous fish to marinate, or serve it in a style worthy of its silver-blue gown, its shiny little eyes, its sharp jaw, its refined fins and its tapering form. It did take quite some time to fish for all these dishes, but here they are, all together.

Before we let you admire them one by one, and before we share with you the many ways of serving herring, it's essential that we tell you a little more about all that comes between the catching and the eating. ⊠

LEFT American importers of herrings in brine took a nostalgic approach, as seen in this painted tin keg, from a firm in Milwaukee, Wisconsin, which based its design on the original wood containers for fish.

OVERLEAF Van Houten, the Dutch cocoa brand, like many other food manufacturers, printed cards like this that were collected by children, as an educational exercise. On the back is a highly detailed text describing the subject represented, followed by an advertisement: "Van Houten, the best drinking chocolate."

Cacao
Van Houten

Banc de Harengs

Clupea harengus L.)

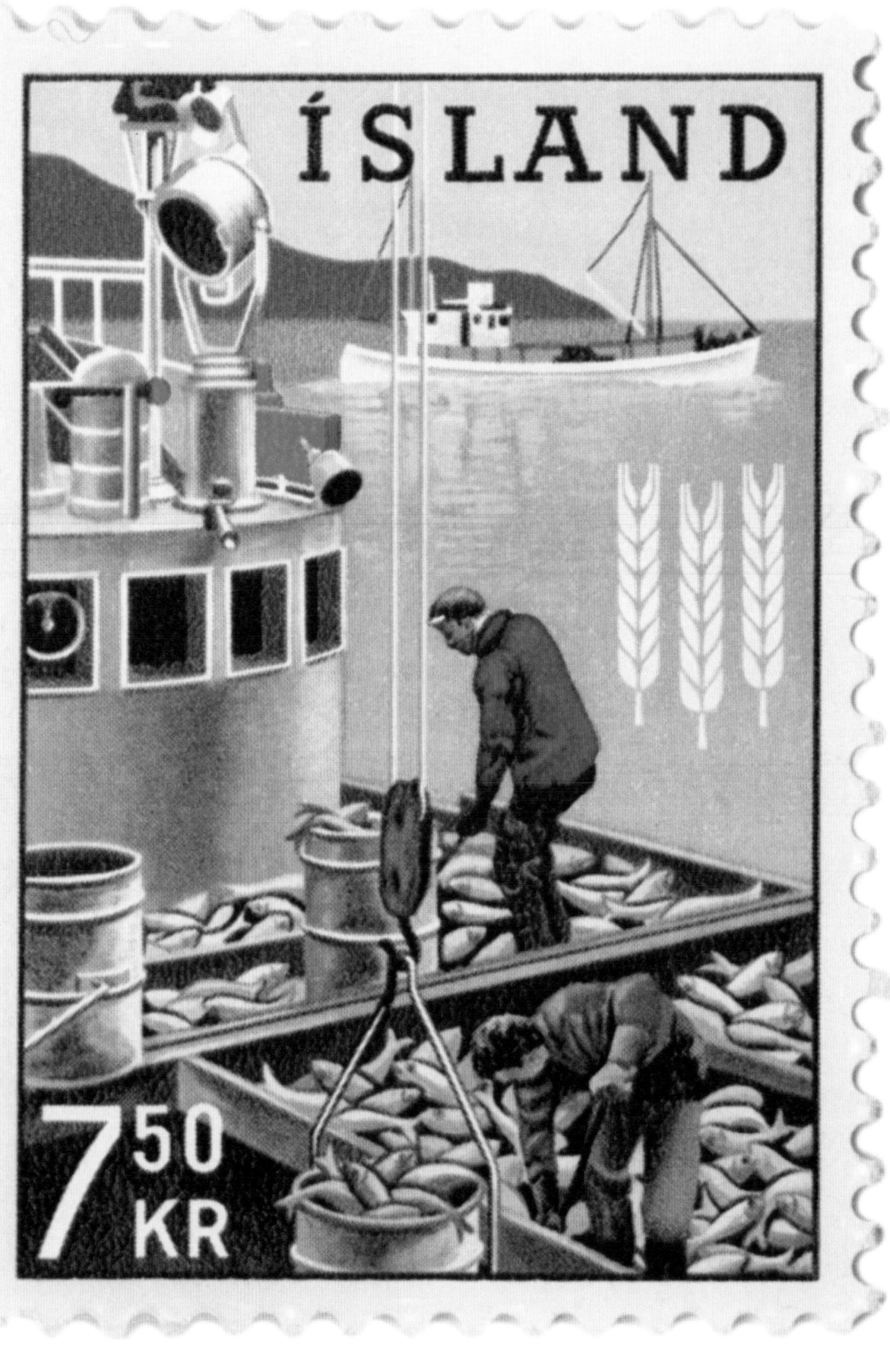
ÍSLAND
7 50 KR

II. A MIRACULOUS CATCH OF FISH

What's the point of telling people that our herring is a member of the *Clupeidae* family, apart from showing off at dinner parties? There isn't any. It's enough to tell amateur zoologists that our fishy friend is a cousin to the sardine, the sprat, and a few other blue-grey fish that swim around in shoals. Hence its name, which is thought to come from *heri*, an old German word meaning, precisely, a multitude, or a host. We speak of shoals or schools (so you can see that this is a subject worthy of study) that are to be found mainly in three parts of the world. You'll encounter the herring, both large and small, wriggling away with myriads of its fellows, in the Baltic, in the Atlantic, and as far as the north Pacific, off the coast of Canada. The waters of the Baltic being less salty, the herrings that swim in it are said to taste different. And talking of food, we humans are fortunate to have to compete only with dolphins, whales, sea lions, and other seals, with gulls and guillemots, and with greedy fish like salmon and cod that make a mouthful of them. It's plain that humans, with their super-efficient deep-sea driftnets that catch tens of thousands of fish at a time, have a clear advantage over all the other predators. In the old days, the job was extremely tough and men risked death at every moment. Nowadays, for herrings as for whales, the odds have shifted heavily in man's favor. It seems the herring species is not quite at ease in completely fresh water, but not in very salty water, either—so the "miraculous draught of fishes" that took place in Lake Tiberias (otherwise known as the Sea of Galilee) doubtless brought Christ's disciples no herrings. And yet there has for ages been something almost miraculous about herring fisheries, especially since the 13th century, when herring salting and smoking began to develop on a quasi-industrial scale. The wealth of the Baltic and the North Sea ports where the Hansa merchants traded kept pace with the growth of Christendom's insatiable demand for this product. Its abundance made it a veritable manna. It is even thought that in Holland, about a million people lived by this maritime activity.

It was said, too, of the city of Amsterdam—whose prosperity in the 14th century was the envy of its neighbors—that it had been built on herring bones! A science called archaeozoology checks on this kind of tale, digging under cities to find out what fish was consumed in them, and at what time. This research has confirmed the presence of herring bones in the Netherlands between the 10th and 12th centuries. So the Amsterdammers' claim is by no means just a legend.

We should not forget that in those days, Lent was widely observed and there were many days of "abstinence." Fish was eaten by both the rich and the poor, and the herring was commonly called Lenten chicken, and sometimes even Lenten ham.

Fish was so important in the marketplace that in wartime truces were sometimes decreed to allow sailors to keep on fishing (yet another miracle!), so that hungry populations could be fed. This occurred frequently during the Hundred Years' War. If there were no herrings, people were sure to go hungry,

OPPOSITE An Icelandic postage stamp bears witness to the fact that Iceland was one of the countries made prosperous by herring fisheries. The little port of Siglufjörður, on a fjord in the north of the country, marketed up to thirty thousand tons of the fish a year.

famine threatened and, who knows, the tide of war could change for the worse. At the opposite extreme, people killed for this fish: In 1429, at the famous Battle of the Herrings, an English convoy bringing supplies, including fish for Lent, was attacked by the French, who weren't at all well organized, being much too busy bickering among themselves. The English hadn't yet seen any Westerns, but they formed a ring with their wagon train and waited for the French. There were many dead, almost all on the French side. As for the fish, which were already dead, history doesn't tell us who ended up eating them. As late as the early 20th century, herring fisheries sustained hundreds of thousands of people. There were boat builders and makers of nets, regular fishermen, and all those seasonal workers who were farm laborers during the rest of the year but who joined in the effort, so plentiful and well paid was the work. Then came the coopers, the salt merchants, the curers, the dealers, the hauliers, and the retailers.

Not to forget the multitude of nimble-fingered women who, as soon as the herring fleet touched land, got to work gutting, cleaning, and salting thousands of fish—sorted by size—and packing them in barrels, while wrapping their fingers in rags to protect them from the sharp blade of their little curved knives. They came from all over the land, even all the way from Scotland, gathering especially at English fishing harbors like Great Yarmouth. On the docks, in the open air, in the street, in all kinds of weather, they would be working non-stop by their benches. Others would repair the nets, while yet others would sell the fish at market, where one can still hear the echo of their booming voices. (And what about the picture-postcard publishers who made a fortune selling hundreds of such seaside vistas?)

The list of all the towns that owed their good fortune to herring fisheries is endless, but in France, Boulogne-sur-Mer, Fécamp, and Beaumont-le-Hareng (on the route of the old horse-drawn carts that rushed wet fish to the inland markets) are among the most notable. In England, Great Yarmouth put three herrings on its first coat of arms, as did Marstrand in Sweden. Like other small towns, Herringfleet —the name speaks for itself—had a Royal Charter in favor of herrings. In Scotland, a rail line was built to Ullapool, solely for the purpose of transporting the fish. In Belgium, there's even a place called Fond des Harengs (meaning Herring Bottom). Guess why. In Germany, the port of Hamburg was founded by Charlemagne in 809 in order to rival that of Boulogne. In Scandinavia, Stockholm made the herring its national dish. Estonia adopted it as its national and regional emblem: Two Baltic herrings float on the coat of arms of the city of Narva. Iceland owes its political and economic independence to the herring —since 1944, thanks to this sea-borne bounty, it ceased to be Danish. As for Denmark itself, it may well be that the Danes still import curry for the sole purpose of garnishing soused herring, an essential ingredient of their traditional Easter meal.

And even if, in modern times, this industry has been transformed, moving elsewhere, even dying out, every one of these towns remains eternally grateful for all they received for so long, thanks to the little silver fish that brought joy and health to their inhabitants.

OPPOSITE An 1884 engraving from the French *L'Illustration* shows the placement of the nets before being cast into the sea. Herrings surface to feed in the evening, so fishing would often take place at night. Once aboard, the catch would quickly be packed into kegs.

LA PÊCHE AU HARENG. — MISE A L'EAU DES FILETS

Mending Herring-Nets.

LEFT No member of a fisherman's family, male or female, old or young, could escape from seamen's work. Repairing nets, when these were made of hemp, was an essential job. This kind of cheap and very simple semi-circular net was often used in Scotland.

OPPOSITE Rectangular nets were used for catching herring. These hung in the water, sometimes with weights at the bottom. Nets varied in form, according to region. Some were fixed structures, forming weirs at the mouths of rivers, especially along the American coasts, as well as in Wales and Scotland. This vintage postcard gives an idea of the damage they suffered.

OVERLEAF A postcard, entitled "Le Havre, arrival of a herring boat," shows the phenomenal abundance of the catch. Some of the fishermen in their oilskins are halfway up to their knees in the herrings that are piled up on the deck, on a boat without a hold.

MENDING THE NETS.   D.F.&C.

C. V. - 2129. - LE HAVRE
Arrivée d'un bateau de harengs

ABOVE This postcard, sent from the English port of Great Yarmouth in 1905, is a reproduction of a painting. It was produced by the well-known postcard publisher, Raphael Tuck & Sons, Purveyor to the Court. The *Oilette Series* to which it belonged often showed scenes from everyday life. Raphael Tuck, an erudite Talmudic student, had emigrated from Prussia to England, where he, among others, contributed to the development of Christmas cards. Tuck's postcards entered millions of homes, where many of their occupants had little opportunity of ever coming into contact with art.

OVERLEAF From St. Ives, in Devon, England, this postcard, sent in 1916, was part of the *Celesque Series* created by the Photochrom Company, an American subsidiary of Raphael Tuck & Sons. The postcards were printed from a black-and-white negative and colored by overprinting the picture using several lithographic stones—one for each color—every single image being retouched by hand, depending on the individual color. Here, yellow is the dominant hue. The scene shows the landing of fish on the quayside as a major attraction.

PAGES 38–39 Mailed from Scarborough, England, in 1913, this postcard is an unretouched black-and-white photograph. The Yorkshire port operated a large-scale herring fishery. The fisher girls (most probably from Scotland) are sorting the herrings by long workbenches with the barrels lined up on the quay, practically in town.

In France, the herring is celebrated every year in Fécamp, Dieppe, Étaples, and of course in Boulogne, and also all along the northwest coast and islands of Sweden: On the isle of Marstrand, on the first weekend in June, it is honored in every imaginable way. In California, the town of Sausalito even organized its first Herring Festival in February of 2013!

Scheveningen, the city Daniel visited as a child, still celebrates the day in May when the first barrel of young herrings arrives: The catch is then put up for auction. In 2012, the proceeds totaled 95,000 euros—for 45 herrings! This was all for a good cause, as this prodigious sum went to a charity in aid of poor children. On that same day, King Herring is offered with great pomp to Her Majesty the Queen (or King) of the Netherlands.

Yet the greatest wonder of all remains that of opening one's mouth wide, holding one of these little herrings (called *maatjes*, and sometimes, in Holland and Belgium, *New Dutchmen*) by the tail and swallowing them whole—without choking or getting one's face all messy. And without swallowing the little Dutch flag that ornamented the *maatje* fillets, which are eaten with bread and onions.

Incidentally, the word *maatje* comes from a Dutch term meaning virgin, because these fish, caught between mid-May and July, have neither soft nor hard roe. That's what makes a truly royal dish of them! Yet we know herring above all as the ultimate plebeian dish, and a Jewish one, in particular. Its first quality, as we've seen, lies in its abundance and the fact that it has always been cheap, so that the poor could afford it in countries situated by cold seas. Once conservation techniques improved and became industrialized, it could be found on the marketplaces of even the remotest *shtetls*. What's more, the herring, as you'll have gathered by now, is a fish. This means that, for both Gentile and Jew, it does not count as "flesh," or in other words, meat. Once you take into account not only the cost of meat but Jewish dietary laws governing the consumption of meat (and not just any meat), you'll readily understand that opting for herring made life easier for mothers who wanted to keep kosher, especially when they were as poor as Job.

Regardless of clichés, it's worth remembering that, not having the right to own and farm land, Jews were often merchants or small shopkeepers. With the arrival of Jews from the Iberian peninsula to the United Provinces (today's Netherlands) at the start of the 17th century, many set up in the herring trade, as importers, wholesalers and middlemen. Once packed in barrels, and also in brine, their merchandise was sent by train to Germany, Poland, and Russia, where local dealers distributed it to markets and grocery stores. Clerk in a herring warehouse: That was the humble job of painter Marc Chagall's father. The job paid him just enough to enable him to feed his nine children. Years later, his son would paint the fish driven from Paradise, flying in mid-air. ⌧

O.S. 418. ST. IVES: SALE OF HERRINGS.

Fisher Girls, Scarborough.

III. THE TRAVELING HERRING

The herring goes where he will, making and unmaking fortunes in the course of his wanderings. When plentiful, he glimmers on the surface of the ocean, to the delight of the fisher folk. In Britain, herrings were even called *"silver darlings,"* a term that reflected both their marketable value, the love they evoked, and the shininess of their scales. In the north of France, people would say, with their inimitable accent, *"Out come the herrings, in comes the money."*

In England, it was the other way 'round. *No herring, no wedding*, so closely did marriages depend on this industry and, indeed, in lean years, the marriage registers recorded not a single union. In fat years, everyone lived off them, including the tailors who sewed the wedding outfits. If the fish disappeared, it was seen as a sign of God's displeasure, and ardent prayers were offered up for their return.

Fishermen followed the shoals closely—their boats would stay out at sea for as long as was needed to catch up with them, sometimes for weeks. They lived on board under what were for a long time very hard conditions. Once the nets had been drawn in, the catch was piled up so high on deck such that the men couldn't move without wading through herrings! Ashore, the women—most of them Scottish—awaited the trawlers' return, but they too followed wherever the fish were to be found. Trains took them, in huge numbers, from one port to the next. It was on this mobile army of thousands of packers that the good conservation of the fish—and so, the fortune of the merchant—depended. In some regions of Britain, up to a quarter of the population lived off this industry!

So it's hardly surprising that so many countries, bordering the Baltic and on both sides of the Atlantic, should have cheered the coming of the herring shoals and enjoyed the bounty they brought. In Maine and Massachusetts, as well as in Nova Scotia, Canada, fisheries developed along the coast and in the river estuaries. There, they piled up branches to build weirs and catch large quantities of *pseudoharengus* known as freshwater herrings or golden *shad*—a species belonging to the great family of the Clupeids. These fish live in the ocean but spawn in fresh water, hence their English name, *river herring*. Latinists will want to remind us that *clupea* is the Latin name for shad, so that our *clupea harengus* is really a shad of the herring type.

Now let's get back to our weirs.

Like so many other things, this fishing technique had been taught by the Indians to the first settlers who, it seems, called the Atlantic Ocean (whose crossing they'd managed to survive) the Herring Pond. Traveling further West, to Alaska and British Columbia, the Pacific herring may still be used as bait for salmon fishing, but the Japanese are particularly fond of its roe, which they import by the ton, to make *komochi kombu*, whose texture is at once creamy and crispy. Long before this trade grew up, the First

OPPOSITE An image for a child's card collection, published by Express Chocolate, whose slogans included: "The best and most practical cooking chocolate" and "The best and most practical of all chocolates to be eaten by hand." The connection with herrings is established by the fact that the Normandy region, which is represented, was one of the major producers of bloaters.

NATIONAL WILDLIFE FEDERATION

WILDLIFE NEEDS YOU

BE A CONSERVATIONIST

ATLANTIC HERRING

NWF © 1978

RIPPER

PREVIOUS PAGES *The Berck Region Coastal Herring Guild*—is represented on a postcard that displays the arms of the ports of Berck-sur-Mer, Calais, Étables-sur-Mer, Le Crotoy, Saint-Valéry-sur-Somme, Le Tréport, and Dieppe. Together, they formed an association for the purpose of promoting the seagoing tradition through one of its products. Their slogan is: "To each his bread, to each his herring!"

THESE PAGES Many countries have acknowledged the source of their prosperity by using images of fish on their postage stamps, together with their Latin names, and sending them off to travel the world.

RENĢE

Clupea harengus membras (Linneaus)

LATVIJA L.DANILĀNS 2005

40

Nations of the North Pacific used to harvest this roe, keeping it fresh on a bed of kelp, to consume at their traditional ceremonies or, when dried, to serve as snacks.

Did you know that before bringing the Pilgrim Fathers from Holland to the coasts of the New World, the *Mayflower* had brought a cargo of herrings to England from Norway? Did the two species share life on board? Doubtless they did, for salt fish was on the list of provisions taken aboard for the long voyage. It may well be that, later on, the tastes of Jewish immigrants from central Europe encouraged sales of the fish, unless it was the plentiful supplies that incited American entrepreneurs to market it in different forms—instead of feeding it to their slaves, or using it as bait for catching cod and lobsters, which were regarded as "nobler" species.

Never mind. Even if, in the United States, people sometimes confuse it with its little cousin, the sardine, and treat it accordingly, drowning it in olive oil and packing it in sterilized cans, the herring still ends up in the kitchens of the entire world. In America, as in Europe, upon attaining the height of its glory, it suffered the fate of all the main consumer products, becoming fodder for advertising men. ⌇

OPPOSITE A black-and-white postcard, sent in 1905 from Lowestoft, another important fishing port in the county of Suffolk, on the Eastern shore of England, shows women packing herrings in kegs or in barrels, and covering them with a layer of salt, which is taken bare-handed from a basin in front of the workers. Once sealed, the barrels were ready to set out on their great voyages.

Lowestoft Fishing Industry—Packing Herrings.

Hope you will like this. Very cold here today.

SCOTCH HERRING CURING.

ABOVE An English card was part of the *National Series* that illustrated everyday activities. Before barreling the herrings, the women who salted them had to grade the fish by size and gut them, emptying the innards from the gills downward. The men were busy hooping the barrels.

3531 Scotch Fisher Girls at Gt. Yarmouth.

ABOVE A black-and-white photograph shows a group of Scottish women at work in the English port of Great Yarmouth. They worked outdoors year-round, and aside from boots and warm clothing, they had to wear headscarves and aprons to protect themselves from the blood and scales.

OVERLEAF A postcard, clearly dated 1905, shows how keenly the herring boats were awaited by women, children, and old men, who were all wrapped up against the cold. Even a dog made the scene!

ndant l'arrivée du hareng.

Collection A. B.

THE HERRING SELLER.

LEFT A fishmonger with her basket is depicted on a 1907 postcard in front of a traditional fisherman's house, with its extra story. All the fisherman's equipment was stored on the ground floor, while the family lived above, never being able to get away from the pervasive smell of fish.

OPPOSITE At the time of this card, dated 1904, herrings were not sold in shops, but by women street vendors who would call out their wares to attract customers. In Scotland, the cry was: "Buy my caller herrin' / They're bonnie fish and halesome farin'!" And in Ulster: "Herrins alay (alive), fresh an' stinkin." Come to the cart and you'll see them winkin'!"

OVERLEAF In times of war, cheap and abundant herring saved many people, as was the case both in Belgium and Great Britain during World War II.
The article that accompanied this press photograph stressed how tired people had become with the fish.

PAGE 56 A 1935 invoice demonstrated the seriousness of the dealer in Boulogne, France, who issued it and guaranteed the quality of his wares. The soused herrings were ordered by a grocer in southwestern France, where they tend to eat more duck than rollmops.

PAGE 57 This American invoice, issued in Baltimore, Maryland, relates to an order for 5,000 herrings. The dealer specialized in the packing and sale of both fresh- and salt herring, as well as herring roe.

CALLER HERRIN'!   D. F. & Co

TÉLÉPHONE Nº 1.69
Ad. Télégr. : SAVOURET

Compte Chèques Postaux : LILLE nº 6.55
R.C. BOULOGNE 2870

Maison fondée en 1905

HOCHART-FOURMENTIN

FABRIQUE DE CONSERVES ALIMENTAIRES
Salaisons en Gros

MARÉE FRAICHE

Spécialité
de
HARENGS BLANCS & SAURS

BOUFFIS - KEEPERS

Filets de harengs Saurs

URGENT : BIEN ADRESSER HOCHART-FOURMENTIN

Boulogne-sur-Mer, le 1ᵉ Avril 1935

MAGASINS & BUREAUX
Place Capécure, 8
BOULOGNE-s/-MER

Doit Monsieur Auguste Blache
Épicerie en gros
Lézignay Corbières
Aude

le montant des marchandises désignées ci-après, payables dans Boulogne-sur-Mer, suivant ordre
transmis par M⁺ Berthomien
expédiées par Maison Goudrant Franco gare Lézignay Corbières
Valeur en mon Mandat au 15 mai prochain.

Marques & Numéros	Quantités	DÉSIGNATION	Prix	Sommes
67	12	bocaux filets de harengs marinés	19	228

Mes bocaux filets de harengs marinés sont
garantis 3 mois date de facture.
Veuillez m'aviser si dans un délai de 6 jours
la marchandise ne vous était pas parvenue.
Les transporteurs devant être rendus responsables
de toute casse, prière de vérifier vos marchandises
avant retrait.

(Voir Conditions de Vente au verso)

C. H. LIGHTHISER

Fresh

Dealer

Salt

Packers of Herring and
Herring Roe

Baltimore, MAY 5 1920

Sold to **M** W L Gross

Brunswick Md

Paid May 10 1920
C H Lighthiser

Roe Shad, each

Buck "   "

5000 cut Herring, per 100 — 1000 — 50 00

Pkge. and Ice:

shipped B. O R R Ft

"HERRINGS FOR NOTHING!"

IV. THE KING'S NAMES

At this point in our tale, it's about time to answer the questions some of you will be asking about the different sorts of herring that appear on the fishmonger's slab, and what they're all called.

By now we know what a *maatje* is, in its Dutch version. It comes onto the market after the "full" herring, whose belly is full of either sperm (soft roe) or eggs (hard roe). There is no sexism here, as both are edible, and have even been restored to a place of honor by leading chefs.

(Because the world's complicated, we'd better nevertheless mention a variety of sweet herring fillets called *matjes*—with just one "A"—in Germany, Scandinavia, and Alsace, France.)

The full herring is fished before the spawning or mating season, between October and January. After that, it is called "spent" or, in French, "*guais*." Indeed, a gay herring. It's much drier then, with not much fat left on it.

Here's how the fishing industry goes about its business:

Once caught, gutted and graded, the herring is salted, tightly packed with its fellows—one layer with the back on top, one, belly up—and kept in kegs. The barrels are small—and the origin of this essential curing technique dates back to the 14th century. It was, it seems, invented by a Dutchman called Beukels, who perfected the art of preserving and barreling, even at sea: Starting with the gills, which are cut off, the fish is gutted, emptied of its innards, but—in the case of *maatjes*, left with the pancreas intact, so that it continues to secrete the enzymes that make the fish tastier. In the old days, after being gutted, the fish was salted and packed in barrels. As for the pancreas, that's what enables the live fish to become fat. So did anyone really think it was going to be simple?

Fat herring? Sure, let's look into that.

You see, the *ne plus ultra* for us who are writing this book is the *schmaltz* herring, or fat Baltic herring. *Schmaltz* is the term used for defining poultry fat, which was carefully preserved to prepare *gribenes* (a sort of chicken dripping). It replaced butter, which is forbidden for cooking or accompanying meat in the traditional kosher Jewish kitchen. It was spread on bread, hence the famous question: "Why is it that when you drop a slice of bread spread with *schmaltz*, it always falls on the side with the *schmaltz*?

Reply of the rabbi consulted: "It's because you didn't spread the *schmaltz* on the right side."

That was a digression. Let's get back to our nice, fat herring, which isn't coated in chicken fat—anything but that! If we say fat, it's just because it has reached maturity and, being really plump, it contains up to 25% fat.

As soon as it's caught, the *schmaltz* herring is soused, meaning that it's covered in coarse sea salt and left

OPPOSITE Royalty, crowned with a wicker herring basket! The 1876 engraving, taken from a newspaper, is very realistic, as one can see the rain falling in fine oblique lines on the basket that crowns a herring seller. The fish, however, don't look very alive. They are bloaters, judging by their stiff bodies and the look of their heads. The vendor is wearing a hand-knitted sweater, like those worn by fishermen. The garments each had such unique knitted patterns that they made it possible to identify a man who had drowned.

Saurissage des harengs à Fécamp. — Dessin de Broux, d'après le modèle de l'Exposition universelle de 1878.

Häringsräucherei.

3080. 4.　　　　　　　　　HERRING

WORKERS.

PAGE 60 This old engraving shows how rudimentary the smoking of herrings could be. The wooden rods on which the fish were spitted can be seen above the fireplace, together with the fishing nets. When a smokehouse became more industrialized, the French called it a *boucane*—a word with the same root as "buccaneer."

PAGE 61 The domestic nature of herring smoking in Germany was displayed in this vintage print. The woman is in the process of taking down the spits on which the bloaters were hung while her cat is taking a close interest in the goings-on.

PREVIOUS PAGES A 1905 postcard with women workers posing at their workplace shows the industrial nature of herring fisheries. The basin of salt into which each worker will reach bare-handed is in plain view. The barrels piled up in the background give a good idea of the scale of both the fishery and the herring trade.

ABOVE A forthright German label claims that the soused herrings sold under the Walkhoff star trademark are "unsurpassed."

to marinate with a weight on its back for about four days. If it has to travel, the contents of the barrel are packed down and, if necessary, covered with a few layers of fish taken from another barrel. Fresh brine is then added, through a little opening in the side of the barrel. Once that has been well sealed, the fish is ready for its last migration.

Before eating a *schmaltz* herring, it is recommended to soak it in fresh water, which is changed at regular intervals, in order to remove the salt. In the case of *maatjes,* which are kept in a light brine, an hour will suffice. After that, it only remains to—guess what?—drown it, in oil, for example. No, not in *schmaltz.* But sugar is often added, especially in Galicia, in Eastern Europe, where there is a taste for sweet-and-sour, especially in Jewish cuisine.

This herring can also be preserved in alcohol, cider, or white wine vinegar, which produces *rollmops*, with fillets rolled around slices of pickled onion or cucumber, the whole thing held in place with a pretty little wooden stick (these days, alas, often replaced with a horrible green or red plastic trident). A variant on these herrings soused in bacteria-killing vinegar is the *Bismarck* herring, which was given its name by a 19th century grocer from the German city of Stralsund, who was a fervent admirer of Chancellor Otto von Bismarck. He sent him a small barrel of them for his birthday, then a second one to celebrate the founding of the German Empire, and so was gracefully permitted by Bismarck to use his name for the product—hence its great success.

There is another common way of preserving herrings: The salt herring is soaked in fresh water for ten days, then drained, carefully dried, and threaded onto wooden skewers. Next, it is exposed to smoke from beech or oak chips for a variable period of time. For a while, anyway.

The result is the bloater or kipper, in French, the *hareng saur*. The word *soor* meant dried in old Dutch, but also referred to *saur,* meaning, in old French, the yellow-brownish color conferred by the smoking process. In the 19th century, the French called the entire business of herring curing *saurisserie*. This used to be a craft or family trade, but in the 20th century it became an industrial process.

– Ever irreverent, the French call herrings salted for at least nine days "*gendarmes*" or "men-at-arms" (perhaps because they're all lined up in a little box?) while the Scots call them Glasgow magistrates (perhaps because they're all so stiff?)

– The word "bloater" speaks for itself. It is a "full" herring, salted and lightly smoked for about eight hours. The process turns it yellow like straw.

– Freshly salted, the French call it "*hareng pec,*" from the Dutch "*pekelharing.*"

– When it is opened on its back side, salted, and slightly cold-smoked, the British call it a kipper or a red herring.

– The *buckling* is hot-smoked whole and salted for several hours.

– And last of all, when it is very, very dry, so that it can be kept for a long, long time, they call it in French "*hareng franc-saure,*" a term and a product for which there's no English equivalent. It has been subjected to twelve to eighteen hours' smoking at between 75.2°F and 82.4°F (24°C and 28°C, respectively), which

HERRING CATCH, KETCHIKAN, ALASKA.

makes it rot-proof—yet still edible, once it's been cooked! Nowadays, the fish is quick-frozen aboard ship before any other processing, in order to avoid the transmission to man of any kind of parasite. (How, I wonder, did they cope with that problem in the old days?)

We nearly forgot to mention a variety called *Surströmming*, maybe because it's not eaten outside Scandinavia. Small Baltic herrings are salted, but not gutted, and left to ferment in a tin can, which will start to deform with the passing of time. It is, it seems, strictly forbidden to open the can inside the house, so foul and tenacious is the smell it gives off. Once the fish has been gutted and washed under running water, it may be served only out-of-doors. For the time being, its importation into France is (fortunately?) rather less widespread than that of Camembert cheese into Sweden.

We really can't complete this great long glossary without mentioning that in English, a red herring means a decoy, something that puts dogs and people on the wrong scent, both in life and in fiction. In French slang, this same red herring, the *hareng saur*, meant a pimp, for these "bloater" boys grew fat on the takings of their *"morues"*—their *cod-girls*, if you like. No doubt his kind tried to take advantage of the honest, if underpaid, "herring lassies," who had barely time to breathe, let alone gossip, while gutting up to forty herrings a minute, which their packer girlfriends deftly barreled. Herring boats may be called dandies or drifters, but they're no tramps. And herring men are no hobos. As for the fishwives of foul-linguistic fame, the French used to call them *harengères*, maybe because of how they *harangued* their customers. ⊞

PREVIOUS PAGES Alaska! Kingdom of the salmon, but also of the herring, highly sought after for fish roe. The birds flying above the boats returning to port loaded with herrings are called herring gulls—an indication of their appetite for their favorite prey. The gulls fulfill a useful function for fishermen by flocking in huge numbers, drawing attention to the shoals near the surface. OPPOSITE The so-called Norwegian technique of pouring brine into a barrel through an opening in its side before completely sealing is depicted in an old photograph. The salt for the brine came from Mediterranean sources, in Cagliari and Sicily, or from Portugal.

Yallop's Series. a 818｜642   Yarmouth Bloaters (Quite Fresh)

OPPOSITE From 1898 onward, the Vita Food Products trademark was extremely well-known in the United States, the company's wares consisting essentially of fish products. A metal container, shaped like the little kegs used in Holland, was meant for the transportation of herring fillets prepared as rollmops, and in this case, marinated in a wine sauce.

ABOVE A typical Great Yarmouth postcard, which was sold in vast numbers, presents something of a paradox as the bloaters are described as being very fresh, but have been put on spits before being lightly smoked using oak chips to preserve them. Smoking turned them a yellow straw color, and not red, as when artificial coloring, which spoiled the taste, was previously used.

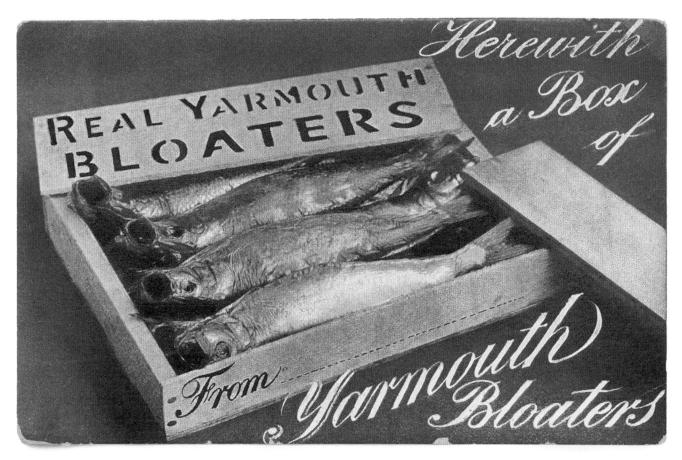

ABOVE On a 1922 postcard, we read "bloaters," a term that most probably originated from the Swedish "blota," or "to soak," as before being smoked, herrings are soused in brine, or simply salted. Boxes like this enabled one to mail the fish or bring them back as a present—thus adding value to the humble product.

OPPOSITE A wooden box marked "Monty Goldberg Kosher Sea Food" was meant for transporting rollmops, and stated that the seafood is kosher—as practicing Jews may not eat crustaceans or mussels. Note that the district on the box is near London's Thames River and Petticoat Lane, where Jews sold (and bought) "wet" (or fresh) fish like herring and carp.

LE PAS DU HARENG

FEET of FISH
ATOMIC DANCE

PAROLES DE
MAURICE
VANDAIR &
SYAM

L'ÉDITION DES VEDETTES
PAUL BEUSCHER
L'ÉDITION DES SUCCÈS

MUSIQUE DE
HENRI
BOURTAYRE
ET ÉMILE
PRUD'HOMME

V. HERRING HUMOR

There is an abundance of jokes and anecdotes about herrings. Here are a couple: A Russian officer and a Jew are sharing a train compartment. At lunchtime, the officer takes a hard-boiled egg from his kitbag and starts to eat it. The Jew takes three salt herrings and a piece of bread from his bag and begins to eat. After he's eaten, the Jew gathers up all the fishbones, wraps them in paper and puts them in his pocket. The Russian officer sees him doing this and says: "Hey, Jew! What do you want to keep all those fishbones for?" "Why Sir, to feed my children: Herring bones contain lots of phosphorus, so our kids become very intelligent, and that's how we poor Jews survive!"

"So, if I ate those bones, would I become more intelligent?"

"Of course you would, Sir!"

"Then give me those bones, Jew."

"Please Sir, not that! That's food for my children!"

In the end, they agree on fifteen rubles. And the Russian starts eating the fishbones while the Jew looks on…

A moment later, the officer stops eating, gives the Jew a dirty look and says: "You thief of a Jew, you sold me these fishbones for fifteen rubles, but those three whole herrings are only worth five!" And the Jew replies: "Bravo! You see, it's already beginning to work!"

There are several variations on this tale, but every one of them goes on about the herring's head or bones, which are supposed to make a Gentile more intelligent, and often, the dialogue takes place on a train, one of those trains that cross the continent for days on end, during which eating makes the time pass more quickly. However, as everyone knows, salt herring makes you thirsty. So here's our next story: An old Jew (another one!) is traveling on the Trans-Siberian. He's very, very thirsty. So he keeps on lamenting: "Oy, am I thirsty! Oy, how thirsty I am! Oy, am I thirsty!"

In the end, the other travelers can't take it any more, so when the train at last comes to a station, someone gets off the train in a hurry and brings the old man a glass of tea and a gourd full of water. He drinks the lot and sighs with pleasure. The train moves on again. The travelers look at one another, relieved by the silence. Only then, the old man starts rocking back and forth again, repeating a new litany: "Oy, was I thirsty… Oy, how thirsty I was…"

And then there's the joke about the fiancée, or the wife. The one that Victor Kuperminc added to his recent translation into French of Leo Rosten's wonderful book, *The Joys of Yiddish*:

A man who couldn't marry off his very ugly daughter goes to see a famous Rabbi in Cracow.

OPPOSITE A 1946 music score cover illustrated with dancing fish skeletons poked gentle fun at American dances, and urged French people to try the *pas du hareng* or herring-step. The lyrics included: *The dance steps from America/ Are fakes, are fakes, are fakes./ Their steps are all eccentrical/ But ours are all French makes./ So come and dance the herring step,/ It's modern and it's sweet./ And when I give the signal/ Kiss your partner on the cheek/ That's all, that's all, that's all (Kisses).*

"Rabbi, I'm desperate because God has given me an ugly daughter," he says to the rabbi.

"Ugly? But how?" the rabbi replies.

"Oh, it's quite simple. If you put her down on a plate next to a herring, you would not be able to tell the difference."

The rabbi thinks for a long time, and in the end, he asks: "What kind of herring?"

Taken aback by this question, the man stops and thinks before replying: "Er… Bismarck."

"A pity," concludes the rabbi. "If it had been a *maatje*, she would have had better luck."

On the French website *www.kitchenbazar.eu*, the taste is different: "If it had been a *schmaltz* herring…"

In France, the great historian Jules Michelet celebrated the herring in his book, *The Sea*, and the poet Charles Cros, who was fascinated by sounds, wrote a text that has left its mark: *The Bloater*. What the herring says may not yet have appeared in any speech balloon—all the same, it has gained a reputation as a "farting fish" that communicates with its fellows by emitting sound bubbles.

In Nice, the red herring's nickname *gendarme* helped turn it into the pilot-driver of a carnival float on the thirty-ninth anniversary of said carnival. The French never miss a chance to poke fun at the *Gendarmerie*. ⊠

OPPOSITE On a card that came in a bar of chocolate, the bloater is a meal for a poor man with dreams of glory. Sadly, a bloater (nicknamed in French a *gendarme*, or "man-at-arms") is all this person, who dreams of being a musketeer, can afford to eat. OVERLEAF Herrings made perfect Lenten fare. This 1913 French card, shows a herring-shaped carnival float during *mi-carême*, or mid-Lent. The celebration made a fun-filled break from the austerities of Lent, when people ate practically nothing but this fish.

CHOLET - Mi-Carême 1913
L'Hareng sort en Carême

Carnaval de NICE XXXIX

REPUBLIQUE FRANCAISE

5c

POSTES

Édition Giletta, phot, Nice.

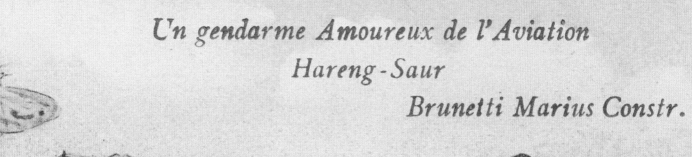

Un gendarme Amoureux de l'Aviation
Hareng - Saur

Brunetti Marius Constr.

Bon appétit !!!

1er " Avril

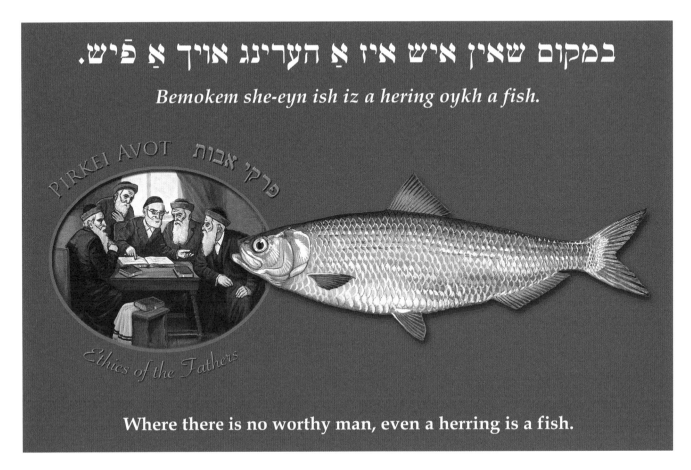

במקום שאין איש איז אַ הערינג אויך אַ פֿיש.

Bemokem she-eyn ish iz a hering oykh a fish.

PIRKEI AVOT פרקי אבות

Ethics of the Fathers

Where there is no worthy man, even a herring is a fish.

PAGES 80–81 A postcard published by the Établissements de Photographie Giletta in Nice, France, dated 1911, uses the same play on words with *gendarme*. The world-famous Nice carnival was the first in history and the first in France.

PREVIOUS PAGES In France, on April 1st, paper fish are pinned onto people's backs as a joke, and the phrase *Poisson d'avril* is happily cried out all day to those who have been fooled in one way or another. This 1908 English postcard is from the *Oilette Series* published by Raphael Tuck & Sons. The words *Bon appétit!* were added in the same pen as wrote the message on the reverse side.

ABOVE A postcard with Yiddish phrasing presents a Talmudic proverb: "Where there's no worthy man, even a herring is a fish." This is a happy blend of: "In the kingdom of the blind, the one-eyed man is king," and "Beggars can't be choosers."

THE SOUTHWOLD EXPRESS - THE GUARD AS A PROFITABLE SIDELINE - PUTS THE DINNERS OF THE COTTAGERS ALONG THE ROUTE · ON THE UP TRAIN - THESE BEING DONE TO PERFECTION BY THE RETURN JOURNEY · THE PROCESS OF CURING THE RENOWNED SOUTHWOLD BLOATERS IS SHEWN

ABOVE This narrow-gage railroad operated only from 1879 to 1929, carrying bloaters from the Suffolk port of Southwold on the North Sea in England. Obviously, the fish was not really smoked as shown here, nor was it sold for the signalman's benefit! Printed on the back of the card, dated 1924, are the words "With our apologies!"

FAYENCERIES de SARREGUEMINES, DIGOIN & VITRY-LE-FRANÇOIS

Siège Social et Service Commercial Central : 28, Rue de Paradis, PARIS (Xᵉ) Reg. Com. Paris 13.370

SARREGUEMINES (Moselle). Télégr. : FAYENCERIES. Tél. N° 7   DIGOIN (Saône-et-Loire). Télégr. : FAYENCERIES. Tél. : N° 7

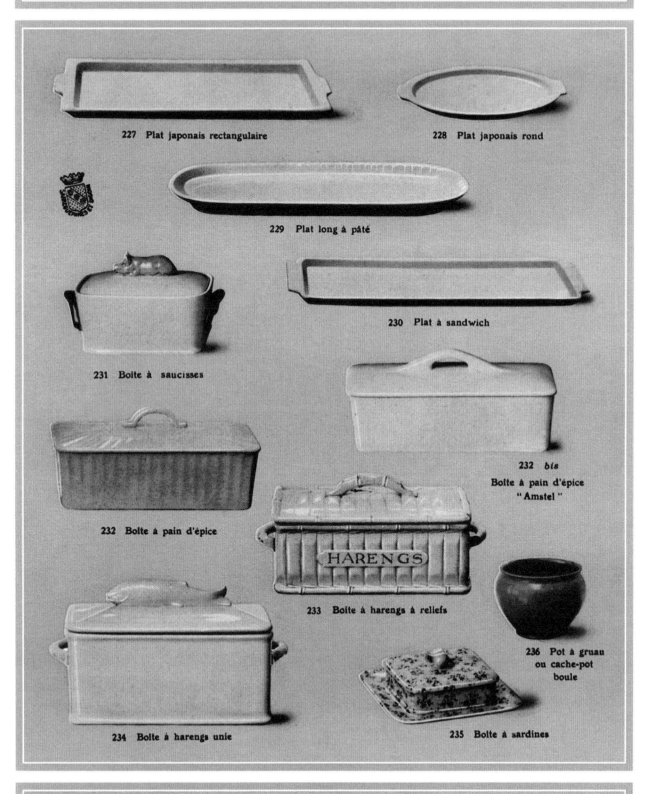

227 Plat japonais rectangulaire

228 Plat japonais rond

229 Plat long à pâté

230 Plat à sandwich

231 Boîte à saucisses

232 *bis*
Boîte à pain d'épice
" Amstel "

232 Boîte à pain d'épice

HARENGS

233 Boîte à harengs à reliefs

236 Pot à gruau
ou cache-pot
boule

234 Boîte à harengs unie

235 Boîte à sardines

VI. THE HERRING TERRINES

From ocean to table, all sorts of industries grew up around our fetish fish, and they have survived to this day. Having more or less covered the main aspects of curing, salting, smoking, preserving, and transporting herrings, we now propose to unveil the rather less-well-known details of the ceramics, in the form of a multiplicity of containers, in which our fish has been served on all sorts of family occasions, including funerals. For is there anything more comforting at times of great sorrow than a piece of herring accompanied by a little glass of vodka? Or indeed aquavit?

Let's turn now to Daniel, and how he made a magical purchase, little knowing that it was to bring about the birth of a collection:

"The first of these herring boxes, also known as terrines, I found in a little junk shop in Cracow, Poland. The place was crammed with objects that evoked another art of living, and in particular *Judaica*, in a country where Jewish culture had long since been eradicated. It was a shock, a real enchantment, to find them all, and with them a whole world of memories welled up before my eyes. Suddenly, I was brought back to my memories, and to those I still have of my mother, who had never wanted to return to Poland. I've always been very sensitive to objects, and especially to the things of daily life. After that, in the course of researching a book I was writing on Central Europe, I was able to ferret out these terrines from the shops and flea markets I visited wherever I traveled.

What I like about this particular object is precisely that it is utilitarian and has no decorative purpose, even when it is decorated. It can take on the most varied forms, and its colored slipware lid may or may not be very realistic. Some terrines, for example, are almost *kitsch*, while others, from the Art Deco period, are very plain and monochromatic. They do really reflect and bear eloquent witness to their periods.

Some of these terrines are extremely sophisticated, and one can guess that they were designed for the tables of the wealthy. An example, on a silver-plated metal stand, is almost a luxury item. But essentially, the herring box is an object that passed from kitchen to table, and even if it was once not so usual in affluent households, kitchen-to-table is how we do it today.

Another point: Their distribution also corresponds to the development, toward the end of the 19th century, of general stores, the ancestors of today's department stores, which took the place previously occupied by street peddlers in Europe. Thanks to growing general prosperity, families would buy chinaware in these shops, and one can well imagine young girls on the point of getting married choosing their kitchen pots and pans and their table china—and, in Jewish families, at least four sets of all utensils, two for everyday use, and another two for the holidays of Passover.

OPPOSITE This page from a Sarreguemines ceramics factory catalog dated about 1925 included various herring dishes and boxes produced at the time. This manufacturer had, from the time of the French Revolution, gained a name as a maker of household china.

When Jews were forced to emigrate to friendlier countries, if they had a few possessions they could take with them and were not fleeing for their lives, they'd organize their move. The silverware and the family china were among the effects that were most carefully packed. We have one fine example in this collection—rescued at just the right moment.

The culinary tradition is one of the main elements of intergenerational transmission, and is particularly central to Jewish culture. Hence our interest in the herring and all that goes with it. I wanted, then, to collect as many proofs as possible of its place in our history."

Let us return now to our collection of herring terrines. The sheer number of items in that collection should help us understand how important these things and the fish they contained were—and still are. The quantity of items collected and the great variety of their styles clearly reveal their makers' skill and creativity.

Most of the large manufacturers in Germany, Luxemburg, and Austria offered terrines in their catalogues. An amusing detail—they were manufactured even for little girls' dollhouses, which all goes to show how basic a part of daily life these things were.

Potteries tended to be located in places where there was plenty of wood (to heat the ovens for firing the ceramics), as well as cheap labor and good infrastructures for transporting the merchandise. These factories sprang up at a time when many small firms switched from craft to industrial production.

Just as today, when the foremost firms commission star designers, entrepreneurs soon learned how to attract the most fashionable creative talents. This was the case with the *Schramberger Majolika Fabrik*, in the Black Forest, which hired the Hungarian industrial designer Eva Ziesel, a star of the Art Deco and the *Bauhaus* eras. Ziesel had a gift for adding a touch of folk art to the pure lines of those styles, and that made her designs greatly sought after.

Some of these factories were, moreover, run by Jews who were forced into exile by the rise of Nazism. Incidentally, when the Nazis took over Vienna, Ziesel herself escaped on the very last train.

The most varied materials were utilized for making these terrines: The finest and most elegant porcelain was used by Villeroy & Boch, for example. Stoneware was used too, sometimes drawing on stoneware clay found near the pottery. This was easy to work and, after being fired, resulted in colors ranging from grey to brown; and *engobe*, a tin glaze, which took very well, made the surface shiny and nonporous. This stoneware was traditionally produced in the Rhineland, as well as in the East of France—at Sarreguemines, in particular. All of which is logical enough for herring terrines produced for mass export to those nearby countries that were major consumers of this fish, none of which were or are Mediterranean countries.

Glass was sometimes used, too, but rather less often, it being more fragile. *Pressed glass*, that is—glass poured into a mold that determined its form and decoration. Some were also made from enameled tinplate, but those will doubtless have rusted with time.

OPPOSITE A vintage Villeroy & Boch catalog page includes various models of terrines from the firm's *Merkur Serie* tabletop line.

Gebäckkasten 3852		20 × 13,5	1,35	1000
„ 3868		19 × 12	1,10	850
„ 3869		17,5 × 11	1,00	680
„ 3935		21,5 × 12,5	1,35	850
Heringskasten 3830	1 2	26 25	1,75 1,50	1500 1050
„ 3967		26	1,75	1070
Käseglocke		23 × 17,5		1050

For the most part, terrines were made of earthenware, because the soft, easily worked material has low production costs. The same goes for *creamware,* a cream-colored variety of the same earthenware. The side of the dish sometimes bore an inscription in German, reminding people what the container was meant for, but in most cases, the surface was plain. The vessel was sober, rectangular, and generally without handles. Lids, on the other hand, were decorated with a design in slip, meaning that they were coated with a sort of fluid paste colored with oxides, which made it possible to create highly sophisticated designs in relief, which sometimes provided a sort of handle. In the case of our terrines, the herring that ornaments them is usually an extraordinarily faithful reproduction of its live model. ⌘

OPPOSITE The design of a number of terrines were inspired by fishermen and fishmonger baskets. This one was made in Wrocław, formerly Breslau, in Lower Silesia, which is still a great center for pottery. The Polish words mean simply "soused herrings."

ABOVE A fine 1920s example of the production of the Paetsch pottery in Frankfurt, Germany, has decoration in the form of faux basketwork and an inscription in Gothic lettering ("marinated herring"). Soon after, the Bauhaus movement was to inspire this factory with more modernist designs.

ABOVE A very large terrine—
14.2- by 6.3- by 5.5-inches—
in the shape of a basket, from
the P. Giesel factory in Breslau,
Germany, dates back to the
very beginning of the 20th century,
before the city became Polish,
as attested to by the Gothic
lettering of the inscription.

MARINIERTE HERINGE

ABOVE A terrine with basketweave decoration was manufactured by the Georg Schmider works at Zell am Harmersbach, in Germany's Black Forest, at the end of the 19th century. On the lid, the fish, in a swimming position, makes a convenient handle.

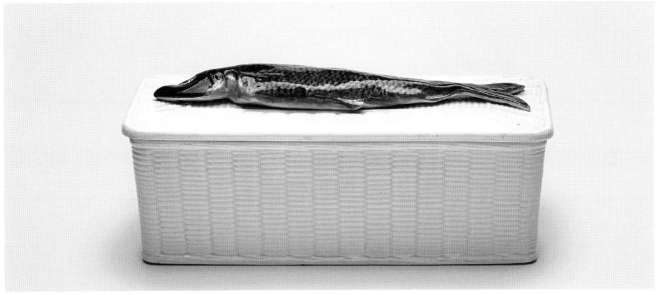

ABOVE This understated example of a terrine inspired by basket-work bears no manufacturer's mark that would enable identification. It was probably made by a German pottery at the beginning of the 20th century. This was often the case with popular items that were mass-produced for inexpensive shops and markets.

ABOVE This very fine example of slipware, made by the German manufacturer Schramberg, in the Eastern Black Forest in Germany at the very beginning of the 20th century, has a polychrome fish and vegetable theme. The handle is in the shape of an onion and stalk.

ABOVE A few decades later, Schramberg produced a two-colored terrine with a highly stylized minimalist design and the purest Art Deco lines in the same kilns.

OVERLEAF The Waechtersbach pottery in Germany, set up in 1832 by Prince Adolf zu Ysenburg, produced this austere terrine, which anticipated the modernist designs of the 1930s.

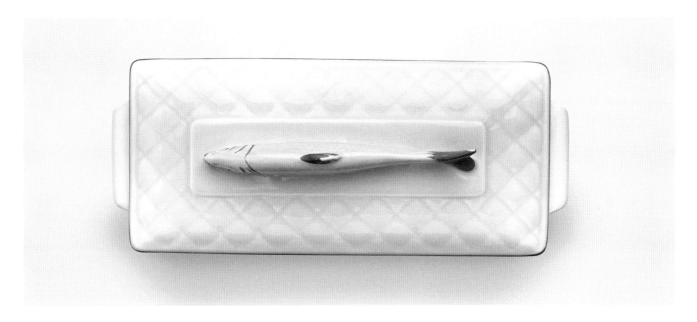

ABOVE The surface of this yellow and red 1920s terrine resembles that of a quilted textile. It comes from the Max Roesler pottery in Dresden, Germany, where production goes back to the end of the 19th century, and which, at the time, had as many as 350 employees.

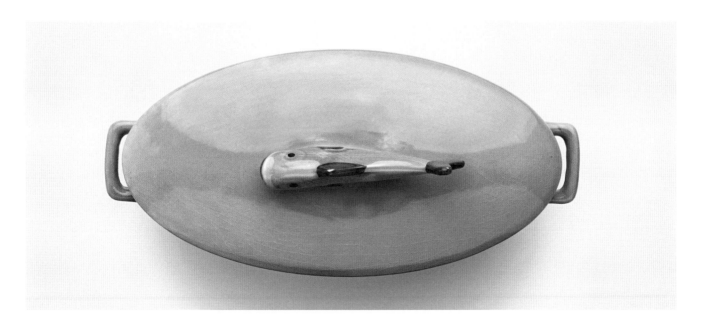

ABOVE This glazed stoneware terrine was manufactured by the Staffel Stoneware Germany in Hesse, in the 1950s. It was produced for trade use and sold primarily to restaurants and catering establishments. A recipe for soused herring was printed on the fish on the side of the terrine.

OVERLEAF The Waechtersbach pottery, founded in Germany in 1832, has always been highly influenced by new styles: Art Nouveau, Art Deco, and Mid-Century. This terrine, with its hand-painted decoration, is typical of the style of the 1950s. The factory is still a going concern.

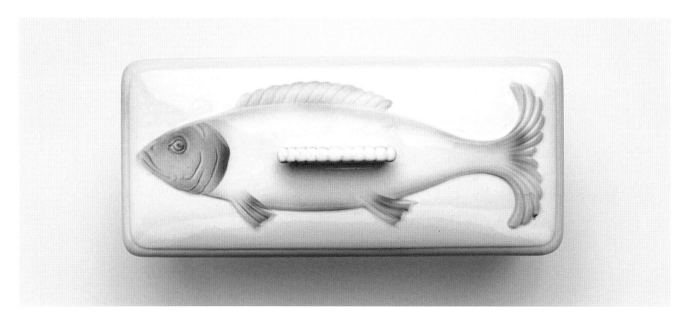

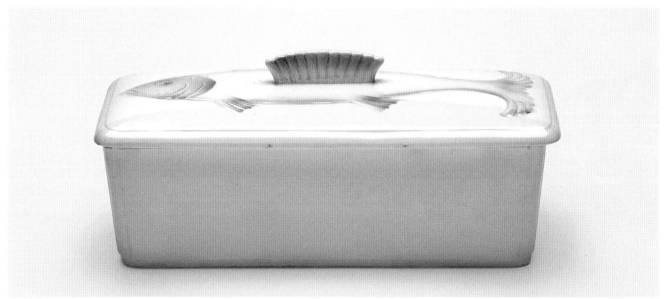

ABOVE This terrine, made by the
Max Roesler factory in Dresden,
Germany, dates from 1920,
when manufacturing was
recovering after World War I.
The lid is decorated with a relief
of a fish in profile, and features
a fin-shaped handhold.

ABOVE The technique used for painting the two herrings on the lid of this terrine is called *Spritzdekor*. It involved spraying color, often with the help of a stencil, producing a blurrier image. This technique was much appreciated in Germany and Austria, and found in objects made by the Wiener Werkstätte, for which Josef Hoffmann and Koloman Moser created designs.

OVERLEAF This terrine belongs to the *Merkur Serie* produced by Villeroy & Boch in the late 1930s at their Mettlach Pottery factory in Germany. It is made of earthenware with a slip finish and is a fine example of the Art Deco and Bauhaus styles.

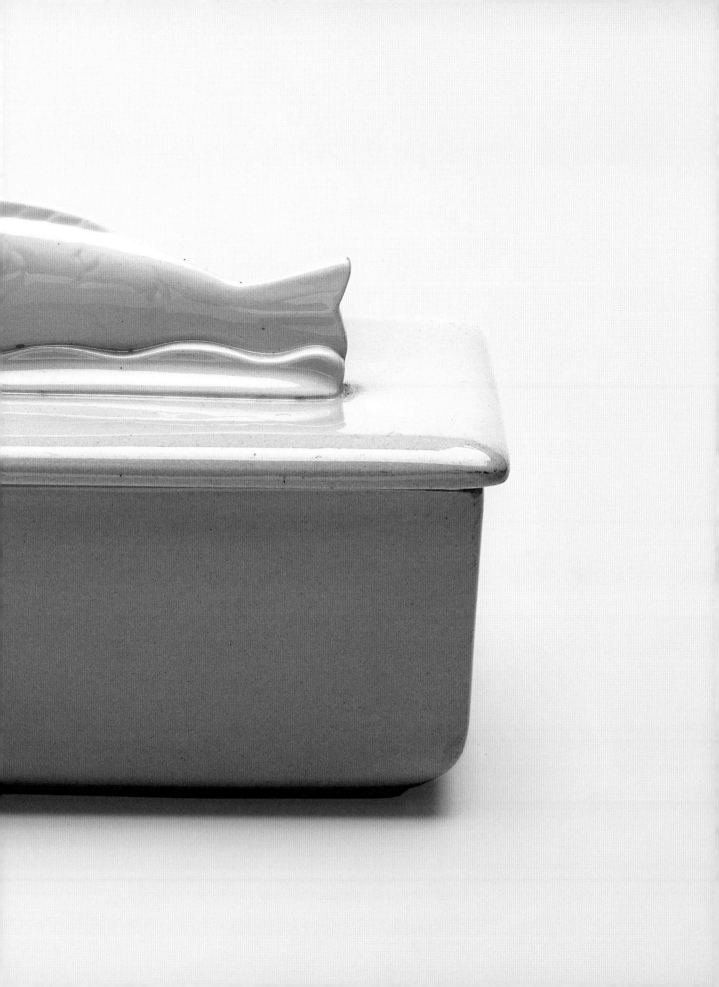

ABOVE The shape of the herring on the lid of this German terrine from the 1930s is highly stylized, and is another example of the *spritzdekor* technique, this time presented in monochrome.

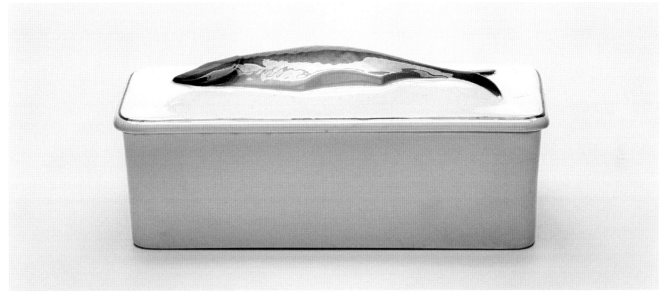

ABOVE Here, the herring on the
lid is realistic. It surmounts a
very plain terrine from the 1950s
whose sole decoration is a thin
red border.

ABOVE An octagonal German
two-handled model is typical of
the 1930s, when several versions
of this design were produced.
The style of lettering used for
the shorthand inscription
is classical rather than gothic.

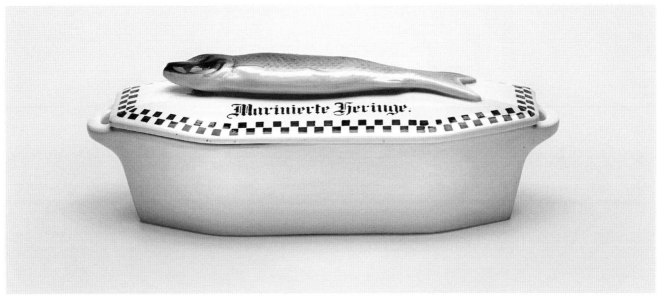

ABOVE While this terrine is in
every respect similar to the one
on the previous page, it has a
more traditional inscription, in
Gothic lettering, with a checkerboard border that recalls kitchen
tiles of the period.

ABOVE This terrine in the Bauhaus style, manufactured by the Staffel Stoneware Germany, in Hesse, in the 1930s, is modernist in form. The handle imitates a scrolled ribbon and the abbreviated Gothic inscription is in a simplified font.

ABOVE This large, enameled tinplate container was made in Austria. The modest, cheap material, which came on the market in the late 19th century, was considered modern and hygienic, until it was replaced by other materials such as Bakelite, and later, plastic. The text in Gothic lettering does, however, anchor it in a very Germanic tradition.

OVERLEAF The sides of this vessel from the 1950s are decorated with a frieze representing fish swimming in a row, making for an unusually decorative effect. The lid has a handle which, for once, is not in the shape of a fish. The abbreviated *Marin. Heringe*, in Gothic lettering, suggests that, at the time, everyone would understand its meaning.

Marin

Heringe.

ABOVE A herring terrine manufactured by Villeroy & Boch is unusual in that it looks like a wooden box. It is oval and its side is decorated with an inscription in Gothic lettering inset against a background in the shape of a label.

ABOVE The fish represented on
the lid of this terrine from the
1920s has very realistic scales.
Its sides are decorated with a
monochromatic frieze of herrings
in relief.

ABOVE The herring on the lid of this oval, footed terrine from the 1920s lies on its belly, which is relatively unusual. The fish also functions as a handhold.

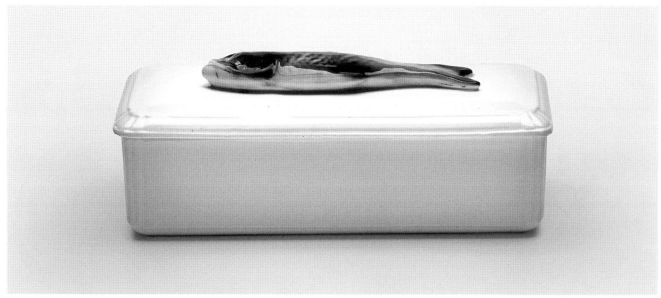

ABOVE What a fat herring crowns this terrine! The lid on which it rests is lightly decorated in the Art Deco style.

OVERLEAF This terrine, a fine example that appeared in the 1932 catalog of the famous Theodor Paetsch Keramik factory, is in the shape of a lifeboat, as shown by its rope decoration and the inscription, Rettungs Boot, on its side.

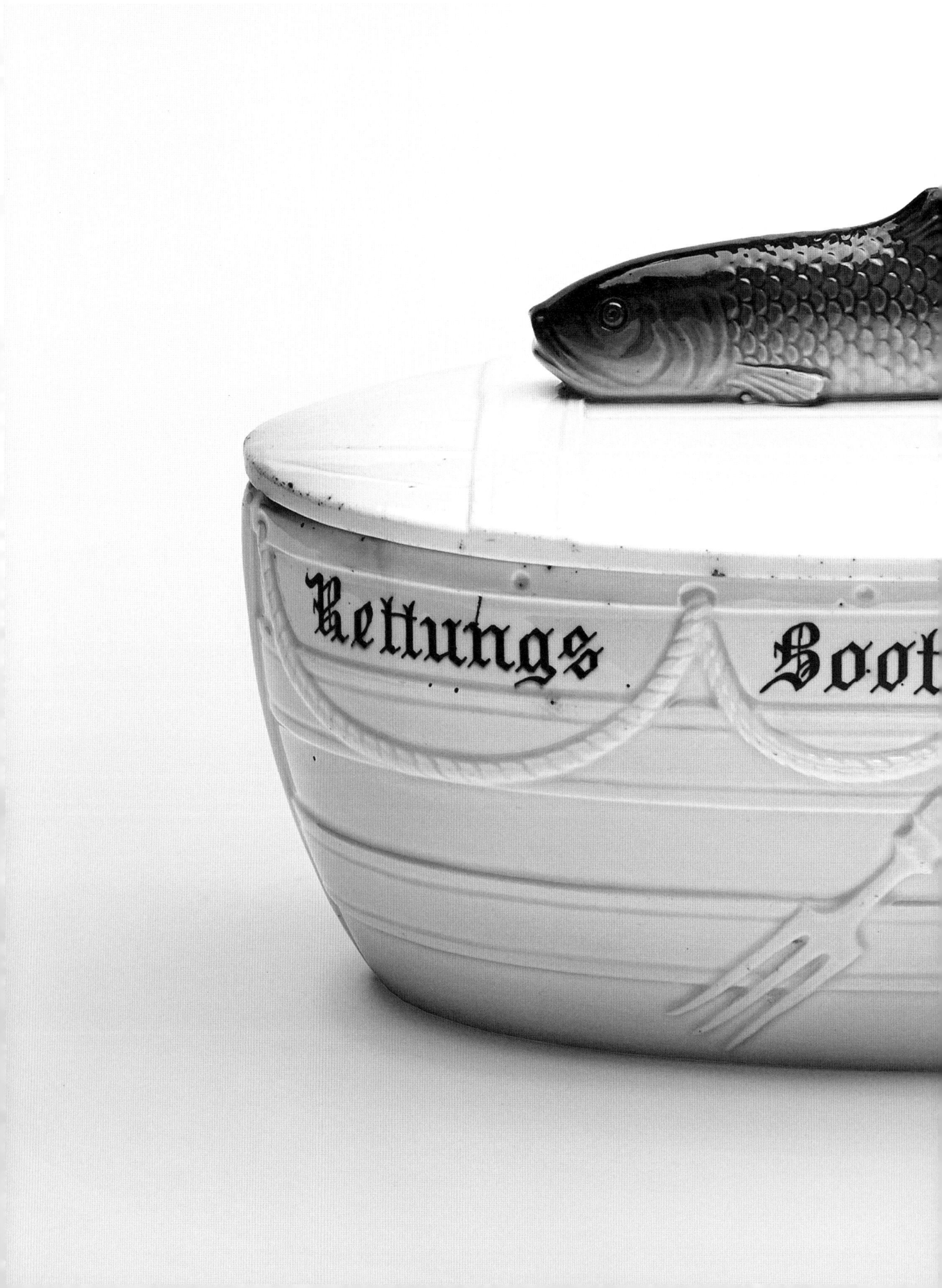
Rettungs Boot

Saurer Hering.

ABOVE The charm of this terrine
from the 1920s lies in the grooves
on its lid. The herring's scales
are very realistic and the fish
is presented in a triple frame.

ABOVE This understated terrine, with its highly realistic decoration and its chamfered lid suggesting a hexagon, dates from the 1930s. It has no manufacturer's mark, but probably comes from one of the many German companies that produced utilitarian china at the time.

ABOVE This terrine comes from the Schwandorf pottery, which is located by the River Naab in Bavaria, Germany. The simplicity of its rectangular form and its ribbed lid show that it was made in the 1930s.

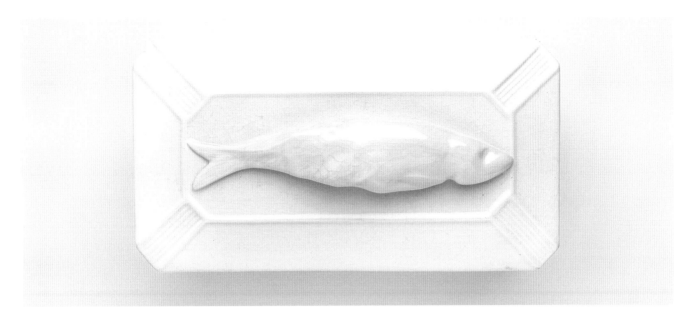

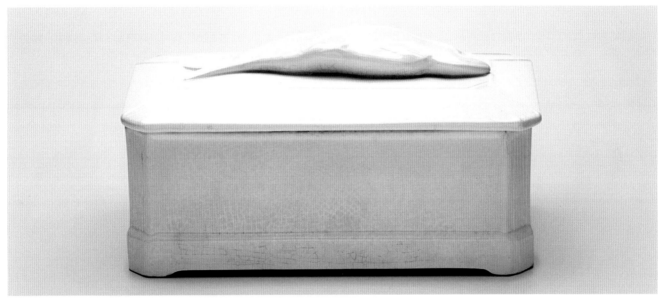

ABOVE This very large
monochromatic vessel in glazed
stoneware measures 15.75
inches. This kind of terrine was
often seen in restaurants and
hotels throughout Germany
and Central Europe in the early
20th century.

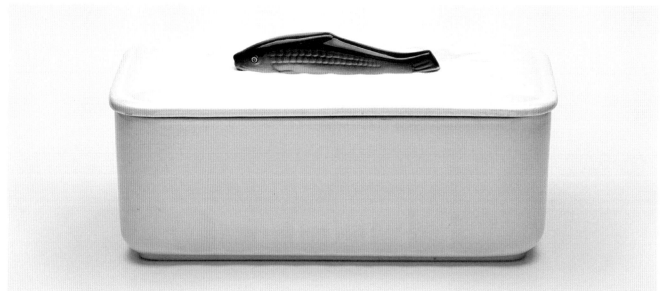

ABOVE The lid of this terrine made at Schwarzenfeld in Bavaria, Germany, represents a very stylized fish, characteristic of the Art Deco style.

ABOVE A terrine produced in the
1930s by Villeroy & Boch at
Mettlach in Germany belongs to
the company's *Merkur Series*.
The fish is not presented on the
lid but appears in relief on the
side of the terrine.

OVERLEAF A rare piece, made of
glass, is a replica of an Art Deco
china terrine produced by the
Schramberg pottery. The
technique is pressed glass, in
which glass is poured into a mold
that determined its decoration.

ABOVE This terrine has rectilinear sides and an unadorned Art Deco look. The herring on its lid is slightly bent, which makes it easier to manage as a handle.

ABOVE It often happened that
several versions of the same
terrines were made from the same
mold, as in this undecorated
monochromatic model produced
by the Waechtersbach factory
in Germany.

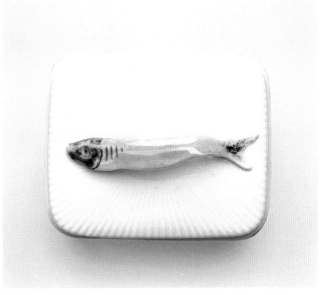

THESE PAGES A series in porcelain consists of four small terrines made by different French factories: Porcelaine de Paris, Betoule et Legrand, and Apilco. They were produced between the 1920s and 1950s.

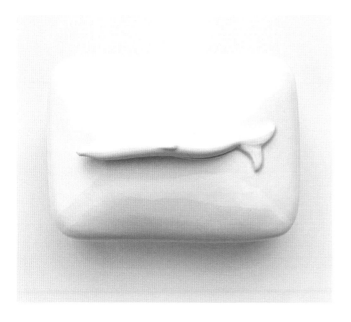

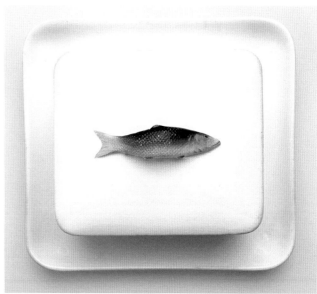

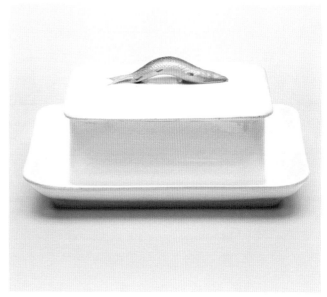

OVERLEAF LEFT This little porcelain terrine made in Flanders comes with its own plate, to which it is affixed. Its decoration, in yellow and black checks, is typical of the 1930s.

OVERLEAF RIGHT This small German porcelain terrine dates back to the beginning of the 20th century. Its special feature is a silverplate stand and handle that shows that it came from a refined and well-to-do household.

VII. THE VIRTOUS HERRING

Like all animals, the human race must have known instinctively what was good for it. A diet that included a herring a day can have had only favorable aftereffects, judging by the energy of the million or so Jews who undertook the exodus to America, the new promised land.

Once there, traditions proved enduring. If we are to believe Professor Jonathan Deutsch, who has written a thesis entitled *Jewish American Food Culture*, herrings have kept their place among the dishes that break the Yom Kippur fast—on *bagels*, of course, doubtless because this fish contains an unimaginable quantity of nutrients beneficial to our health (especially after those 25 hours of fasting), as confirmed by recent scientific research. But the Flemings already knew that, and it has been borne out by their saying: "When herrings abound, the doctor's homebound." Let's admit that adage was rather more flattering for the fish than the German proverb: "If you can't pay for herrings, don't hanker after trout!"

Well, as they say, about the only thing it can't do is speak—but forgive me, I was forgetting to say that the herring is as dumb as a carp, which doesn't prevent it from having a multitude of other qualities. So let's make a list of them.

Taking its virtues in any old order, our herring is rich in:

– Omega 3s, powerful anti-inflammatory agents, the very mention of which is enough to cure all ills. In particular, moodiness and depression (brought on by prolonged fasting, as already mentioned).

– Amino-acids—nine in all, essential for the formation of our digestive enzymes (no, herrings are not indigestible, any more than the onions that accompany them!) and for renewing tissue, like skin and bones. It also promotes the formation of hormones, which all goes to explain the large families you'll find in Daniel's and my family trees—and that of the Expressionist artist Chaim Soutine, the tenth of eleven children.

– *Docosahexaenoic acid,* more commonly known as DHA, which plays a part in the brain's development and functioning, and the maintenance of cognitive function and vision. You see, our Jew on his train was quite right! Note in passing that DHA is also an important constituent of the testes and sperm, but that's really just a detail. Our fishbone salesman wasn't going to take his boasting any further, and in any case recent studies show that the regular consumption of Omega 3 sharply lowers aggressivity.

And last but not least, the herring contains selenium, which prevents premature cellular aging: This substance keeps our man (or woman) young and energetic, ever ready to make a fast getaway to America if there's a pogrom, or go till the soil of the Promised Land. Those are just two examples to illustrate its virtues.

OPPOSITE *Still Life with Herrings*, a 1916 oil on canvas, was painted when the artist Chaim Soutine, who was born in a *shtetl* in Belarus, was living at *La Ruche*, an artists' colony in the 15th arrondissement of Paris. OVERLEAF An oil on cardboard, by the Ukraine-born painter Abraham Mintchine, represents three herrings on a dish, a cup, and a loaf of *challah*, the bread eaten in Jewish homes on Friday evenings for *Shabbat*. PAGES 140–141 "If you can't afford herrings, don't go hankering after trout," is a German proverb with a reality-based message that can be perfectly applied to these paintings. Soutine and Mintchine suffered extreme poverty when they were living at *La Ruche*—and if only a herring was on the menu, it was considered a feast!

elui qu

se payer

ne doit pas dé

Prov

ne peut pas

Harengs

irer de Truites.

rbe Allemand.

As a postscript, we absolutely cannot pass over the fact that the scales are used in cosmetics; they make lipstick and nail varnish brighter. For women, a real morale booster.

Yet in another miracle, the herring even brings together the environmentally minded and the fashionable bohemians.

A small ecological plus, for the herring is one species that is not on its way to extinction. Quite the contrary. After an alert in the 1970s, and even if the stock remains fragile, it is still, thanks to sustainable fishing, one of the most abundant fish in the sea.

A dish for princes up to the 14th century—when, barely covered with a thin layer of salt and straw and conveyed on horseback by the wholesale fishmongers, "powdered herring" arrived in Paris almost fresh —it was later to become the poor man's banquet. Popularized by Ikea all over the world in the late 20th century, the ordinary *clupea harengus* has now become one of the ultimate "in" foods. Very recently, it resurfaced in San Francisco Bay, where the local chefs have made a hit of it. It will be found today in our cities, wherever the fashion-conscious are revisiting traditions with discernment and a concern for style. In Paris, they get up early to raid the stalls at the Richard Lenoir market for all kinds of herrings. And in New York City, the appetizing establishment of Russ & Daughters is the *crème de la crème*. Customers rush back to their lofts, loaded with fillets to serve as *smorgasbord*. Accompanied by fingerlings, or the even more tender Mona Lisa potatoes and (it goes without saying) washed down with vodka or *Schnapps*, herrings have taken over from sushi and sake, blinis and smoked salmon—both of which have suddenly lost much of their allure.

Ultra-sophisticated versions of the traditional French brasserie's herrings in oil accompanied by potato salad are now making an appearance on the chicest brunch menus—and who knows if we'll not be seeing them any day now, even in the South of France, swimming in the middle of a *pan bagnat* flatbread, from which they have ousted their cousin, the anchovy?

So, to those pork addicts who claim that there's not a rib to be spared in a pig, we'll answer loud and clear that our grandparents' herring is fascinating, appetizing, nourishing and, when all's said and done, the height of cool. ⌗

OPPOSITE "Now especially tasty" proclaims the German poster for these herrings, which aren't green but young, and so endowed with every virtue. They were also supposed to permit all forms of licentiousness, as it was from the herring sperm (the soft roe or milt) that AZT, the first anti-AIDS remedy, was extracted, before the molecule was obtained synthetically—and doubtless far less tasty than the marinade intended for the pretty blue terrine with its lovely decorations that sits in the background of the poster. OVERLEAF LEFT A 1959 photograph illustrated a tradition begun in 1402 by a famous pirate, Klaus Stortebeker, in the city of Verden, in Lower Saxony: Before being executed, he requested the setting up of a foundation to feed the town's poor. So 800 salted herrings were distributed every year at the same period, together with rye bread, in the courtyard in front of the town hall. But possibly this is just a legend. OVERLEAF RIGHT This original illustration comes from an educational textbook issued in 1960 by the Royal Institute of Natural Sciences in Belgium. It shows very clearly what becomes of the herring once it has been caught.

fish music food community

Sausalito Herring Festival

FEBRUARY 9, 2013
11am - 4pm Gabrielson Park
by the Ferry Landing, Downtown Sausalito, CA

Cass Gidley Marina
Sausalito Community Boating Center

cassgidley.org

The delicious Scheveningen Dutch Herring Arriving June 5th. But hurry, they're not here for long.

The Authentic **Double Dutch**

Dutch Herring & Genever Gin

LEFT Even California is embracing the herring! At this American festival, many restaurants and chefs create original herring recipes. Information about the San Francisco Bay area, the benefits of eating fish, and the fishing industry are available. All profits go toward turning the Cass Gidley Marina into a boating community and education center.

LEFT BELOW In New York City, every year, the famous Grand Central Oyster Bar and Restaurant in Grand Central Station celebrates the arrival of *maatjes* from Holland.

OPPOSITE The painted brick facade of the popular *Aamanns-Copenhagen* restaurant in New York City announces that traditional Scandinavian dishes, including herring, are on the menu. People also go there for an assortment of prepared dishes, like their famous *smørrebrød*. The parent restaurant is in Copenhagen, Denmark.

OVERLEAF The establishment that was to become the famous Russ & Daughters was opened in 1914 on the Lower East Side of New York City by Joel Russ, a poor Jewish immigrant from Galicia, in Eastern Europe. The shop's unusual name is due to the fact that it was subsequently taken over by the women of the family. For a long time this store was frequented by the local, sometimes poor, residents of the neighborhood, but now it has become the last word in trendiness. Run by the fourth generation, Russ & Daughters still sells, among other delicacies, herring of all kinds, including rollmops, *maatjes*, chopped, in salad, in cream, or in a mustard and dill sauce.

VIII. TRADITION! TRADITION!

Before we get down to work on our herring recipes, let's make a quick round of various contries, to see what customs and eating habits have grown up around the herring: The Scandinavians and Finns eat herring all year 'round, but especially at Christmas, at Easter, and in June, to celebrate *Midsommer*—the arrival of summer. They like to accompany it with sour cream, dill, hard-boiled eggs, rye bread, and *snaps/Schnapps*, or aquavit—strong spirits that are variations on the vodka theme. In Sweden, a thick soup is served in winter based on barley and bloaters. Herring stalls serve dozens of different varieties, as well as breaded and fried herrings, along with mashed potatoes, cranberry jelly, and cucumbers.

In Norway, herring has been on the domestic menu since 600 BCE, as proven by the famous fish bones… And since Jesus came on the scene, herrings have been served for Christmas, when they are generally filleted.

In Finland and Denmark, herrings are celebrated with national festivals, during which they are served in a multitude of forms. In Denmark, at a competition organized at Hvide Sande, one must wait until April for the fishing to start. Enthusiasts come from the Netherlands and Germany, as well as from all over the country, and eat herring at all hours.

In the Ukraine, herrings are one of the 12 dishes served on Christmas Eve. With vodka, of course.

In Poland, they are on the menu for Easter breakfast, together with a large variety of salads and beets. They are also one of the 12 Christmas dishes. The traditional *Śledzie* recipe includes rollmops mixed with finely chopped apples, onions, and hard-boiled eggs, to which have been added sour cream, lemon juice, garlic, and pepper.

A variant on this recipe is one of the best-known items in Jewish cuisine. It's called *forschmak,* meaning foretaste—which is logical enough since it's served as an appetizer, sometimes at *Pessah*, or Passover, on pieces of matzoh, unleavened bread.

In the Netherlands, when herrings are not gobbled down on the street, in a typical gesture, or eaten in a little roll called a *broodje*, which has been filled with finely chopped sweet onions, *maatjes* are served with baked potatoes, runner beans, bits of bacon, and onions.

In Germany, they're to be found in all the bars, and in Berlin it's still customary to serve rollmops at a *Katerfrühstück,* an anti-hangover breakfast. It's thought to be lucky to eat them at midnight on New Year's Eve. The herring is a symbol of plenty, one in which the Poles and Scandinavians still believe.

In Britain, the English preferred bloaters to kippers. For the Scots, it was the other way round. As we've seen, both peoples ate them for breakfast, but also, for "high tea," the British evening meal: Kippers for tea was essentially a working class custom, hence the disdain of the maîtres d's at elegant restaurants when

OPPOSITE Boulogne-sur-Mer is still France's main fishing port. On this poster, French pride is symbolised by the colors of the French flag—*bleu, blanc, rouge* (blue, white, red), which are associated with the trademark of this brand of fish preserves. It's unusual to package herrings in a can, even if this is done in the United States, where herrings are sometimes sold as sardines. In any case, sardines, pilchards, mackerel, and herrings themselves all belong to the same family and have the same traditions.

someone requested them later than breakfast. In Ireland, people would get thoroughly fed up with the Lenten diet, so that once Lent was over, they would hold funerals for herrings. What they did to the fish before this ceremony remains a mystery.

In Russia, they prefer to bury herrings under a thick layer of mayonnaise and vegetables. The dish is called "herrings under a fur coat." In the Philippines, dried herrings are served for breakfast, accompanied by garlic rice and hard-boiled eggs – after which, one can face any typhoon. In Jamaica, they eat a dish called *Solomon Gundy* (a term that probably comes from the French *salmigondis*, meaning "hodge-podge"). It's a sort of red herring to which red pimento and other spices have been added. It's also canned for export. This "hodge-podge" is served with crackers.

Curiously enough, the same term, *Solomon Gundy* is used in Nova Scotia for rollmops. Some say that the recipe was introduced by the Germans; others believe that it came in with Jews from Europe. Could they have been the same people?

In Canada, the land with the world's one and only herring university—*The Herring School* (in British Columbia)—not content with studying the herring from all aspects, also exports it to the whole wide world, including Haiti.

In Haiti, too, they don't turn up their noses at bloaters. They mix them with scrambled eggs spiced up with hot sauce. First the fish is chopped up into little pieces, *en chiquetaille*, then pimentos, onions, garlic, and lemon juice are added. The mixture is then fried in oil and served on bread. In the eating, they call it *chikaye d'aran sor*.

In Japan, they make herring sushi and sashimi, which can be eaten at all hours. The same goes for roe —*kazunoko* in Japanese. There, too, the symbol of prosperity comes into its own, as the dish is served on New Year's Day. This demand for herring roe, imported from Alaska, enriches the enormous trawler fleet which, like a highly disciplined army, is deployed every year near Sitka, closely monitored from the sky by helicopter pilots. Never mind that these ungrateful pilots prefer to eat salmon. Fortunately, the descendants of the Tlingit people have kept their taste for herring roe on seaweed, which they offer one another. One could call this delicacy "the wise man's caviar."

And what about France? Well, the French never need a pretext to treat themselves. Herring has always been so much a part of life that you can find it even on the little cards that came with chocolate bars. Children used to collect them and stick them in albums. But as for serving the fish with cocoa, that's too much of a reach, even for a Frenchman! So we'll make do with the more traditional recipes that follow. ⊠

OPPOSITE The fishing boats on this little educational card are called drifters. On the back of the card, it says: "To collect these pretty pictures, buy from your supplier the album 'North America,' published by the delicious Chocolat Pupier." OVERLEAF LEFT A color lithograph obtained by printing different colors, by applying separate stones to a press—was part of a series of images to be collected by children. OVERLEAF RIGHT This color print for Chocolat Ibled dates back to the beginning of the 20th century.

CHOCOLAT PUPIER

PECHEURS DE HARENGS

CHOCOLAT FÉLIX POTIN

LE HARENG

LES HABITANTS DES EAUX.

CHOCOLAT IBLED

PARIS — MONDICOURT

HARENG QUI GLACE HARENG NOUVEAU

A TRAVERS LES FLOTS

CLASSE DES POISSONS
1. Grondin. (Rouget)
2. Hareng.

Edition de la CHOCOLATERIE D'AIGUEBELLE (D

Le Monde Sous-Marin.

1

2

(ne)

Madrépore protée.

Maine **SEA**

PACKED BY L. A. FISH &

h's

NET WT. 15 OZ.

SALT AND WATER ADDED

IERRING

O., JONESBORO, ME.

SEA ★ Bran

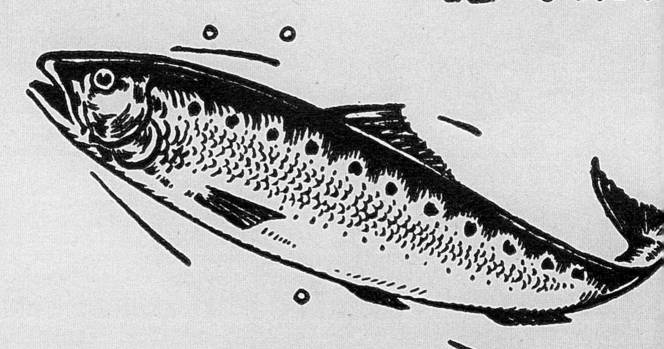

Ocean
HERRING
WITH SALT AND WATER ADDE

CONTENTS 15 OZ. AVOIR.

OCEAN HERRING
SALT AND WATER ADDED

PACKED BY
R.B. & C.G. STEVENS
JONESPORT, MAINE

PAGES 156-157 On this image for collectors, the herring appears next to a red snapper, as the two fish were sometimes confused with one another, although the red snapper lives in warmer seas, notably in the Mediterranean.

PAGES 158-159, 160-161, AND THESE PAGES The series of six canned herring labels illustrates a variety of preparations. The packaging mirrors the different styles of the periods in which they were created: Art Nouveau, Art Deco, and the 1950s.

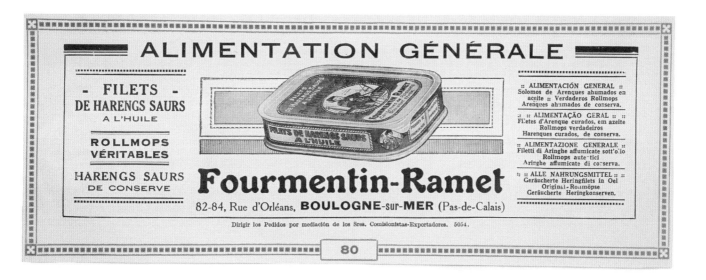

OVERLEAF In the late 19th century, French schoolchildren were already advertising targets, as seen by this piece of blotting paper (for when people wrote with pens and ink) that touts the qualities of Simon rollmops. Simon was a company in the Pas-de-Calais, in Normandy, France, founded in 1886. The brand was also doubtlessly targeting adults.

PAGES 166-167 Little recipe books like these were distributed in England by the Herring Industry Board—that had been founded in 1937—to help the fishery business and encourage consumption of fish. They often offered advice on how to gut, slice, and fillet the fish, and suggested various ways of preparation—some, as here,

for summer meals. Amusingly, there were recipes for every hour of the day, for breakfast, for lunch, for tea, or high tea, the British evening meal, but also recipes for invalids and babies.

RECETTES

Le **Rollmops "SIMON"** se consomme nature tel qu'on le sort du bocal : soit en Sandwich, soit avec une salade de haricots ou une salade de pommes de terre, soit encore avec des pommes de terre cuites à l'eau ou des frites.

ROLLMOPS SIMON
23, Rue Christophe-Colomb - WASQUEHAL (Nord)
TÉLÉPHONE ROUBAIX 73-36-77

OPS "SIMON"

N'oubliez pas que tout bon hareng de qualité préfère terminer sa vie dans un bocal de **ROLLMOPS "SIMON"** plutôt que dans le ventre de la baleine.

IMPRIMERIES JOMBART FRÈRES LILLE - PARIS

WHEN YOU'RE USING THE OVEN—
POP IN KIPPERS OR BLOATERS

Lunch - Bag Bloaters

1 Bloater per person.
Lemon juice.
Bread and butter.
Pepper.

Split the bloaters open and take the flesh off the bones in long fillets. Season with pepper and a squeeze of lemon juice. Place on a greased fireproof dish, cover with a lid and bake in a brisk oven for about 8 minutes. Place the hot fillets between slices of bread and butter. They make really wonderful sandwiches to eat while hot or later when they are cold.

LUNCH-BAG BLOATERS

Summer Kippers

Wrap as many kippers as you want to cook in greaseproof paper, or put them in a covered casserole. Bake for 10 minutes.

Special Herring Recipes for

JULY

Made in minutes · **Cucumber cool**

Looks really summery · **Good food**

A complete summer diet in itself

CHOPPED HERRING

SONIA ROZENSZTROCH'S RECIPE

INGREDIENTS

2   herring fillets

1   apple, peeled

2   slices of bread, soaked in water then pressed between the hands

2   hard-boiled eggs

3   tablespoons vegetable oil

1   tablespoons vinegar

1   teaspoon powdered sugar

1   tablespoon chives or scallions, freshly chopped

DIRECTIONS

1. Mix the herring, apples, egg whites, and bread.
2. Add the oil, vinegar, and powdered sugar, and mix for a few seconds.
3. Place the mixture in a shallow dish, preferably in the shape of a fish, and decorate the top with hard-boiled egg yolks mashed with a fork and scallions.
4. Serve chilled with rye bread.

MARINADE OF SMOKED HERRING FILLETS

SONIA FIDLER'S RECIPE

INGREDIENTS

2 packages smoked herring fillets, approximately 6-8 fillets

2 small or one large onion, cut into rings

2 bay leaves

2 carrots, cut into round slices

$7/8$ cup (100 g) powdered sugar

$1^1/_3$ cup (330 ml) wine or cider vinegar

$1^1/_3$ cup (330 ml) of water

2 whole cloves and some grains of black pepper

DIRECTIONS

1. Arrange the fillets in a shallow dish, and cover with milk.

2. Leave them to desalinate for an hour or two. Take them out, rinse them under water, and dry them on paper towels.

3. Boil the vinegar, water, and sugar with the carrots for a few minutes, until the sugar is dissolved.

4. Arrange the fillets in a lidded dish or similar container. Arrange the onion rings in layers or on top of the fillets.

5. Pour the boiled mixture over the fillets and onions, then add the bay leaves, pepper, and cloves.

6. Let cool, then refrigerate for two to three days before serving.

OPPOSITE This postcard, illustrated by Jean Paris, was part of the *Our Regional Dishes Series* published in 1910. Vegetables, desserts, and fish and crustaceans were represented on different cards. On the back of this particular one is a recipe for fresh grilled herrings in mustard sauce, and a handwritten message: "Get your teeth into these good herrings."

LES HARENGS FRAIS GRILLÉS

MARINATED HERRING
WITH DILL

INGREDIENTS

4 very fresh herrings, cleaned

2 cups (500 ml) wine vinegar

½ cup (120 g) brown sugar

1 teaspoon black peppercorns

1 teaspoon allspice

3 bay leaves

1 bunch of dill, coarsely chopped

3 red onions, cut into rings

2 carrots, cut into round slices

DIRECTIONS

1. Boil the vinegar, sugar, and peppercorns in 1 cup of water for a few minutes.

2. Turn off the heat. Add the allspice and bay leaves.

3. Let cool.

4. In a bowl, add the herring (cut into chunks), the dill, the onion, and the carrots.

5. Pour the cooled liquid over, cover, and refrigerate, preferably for three days.

6. Serve with boiled potatoes and sour cream or potted cheese.

HERRINGS IN CREAM SAUCE

OPPOSITE AND PAGES 176, 179, 180, 183, AND 184 Advertising stickers for Berlin-style rollmops proclaim them as being a miracle hangover cure—thanks to their acidity. These rollmops became popular in Germany in the 20th century, but were also appreciated in many other countries. The *rémoulade*, a mayonnaise to which mustard, aromatic herbs, capers, and chopped baby cucumber pickles are added, is surely less dietetic than the herring it accompanies.

INGREDIENTS

2   cups (400 g) smoked herring or rollmops

1   cups (200 g) sour cream

3   shallots or one large onion

1   apple, sliced

    juice of one lemon

1   teaspoon of white vinegar

3   dill or sweet and sour pickles

1   teaspoon chopped dill and a few dill sprigs

1   pinch of pink peppercorns

    pepper

    milk

DIRECTIONS

1. Arrange the herring fillets in a shallow dish and cover with milk.
2. Let them desalinate for 1-2 hours.
3. Take them out and rinse under the tap and dry them on paper towels.
   This step is useless if you are using rollmops.
4. Peel and slice the shallots or the onion.
5. Cut the large pickles into slices.
6. Arrange the herring in a terrine. Cover them with lemon juice and vinegar. Add pepper.
7. Add the slices of apple, the pickles and the chopped dill.
8. Cover with the sour cream, and stir well to completely coat the fillets.
9. Sprinkle with sprigs of dill and the pink peppercorns.
10. Marinate overnight. Serve with rye bread and boiled potatoes.

HERRING MARINATED IN BEER

INGREDIENTS

2   packages sweet smoked herring, approximately 6-8 fillets

2   sweet onions (or a bunch of scallions), cut into strips

1   teaspoon juniper berries

2   bay leaves

    ground peppercorns

1   bottle of beer, preferably Belgian

DIRECTIONS

1. Arrange the herring fillets in a terrine.

2. Cover with the onions, add juniper berries, bay leaves, and pepper.

3. Pour beer over the herrings and marinate in the refrigerator for three days before serving.

HERRING MARINATED IN OIL

INGREDIENTS

2   packages smoked herring fillets, approximately 6-8 fillets

2   cups (500 ml) milk

2   red onions, sliced

2   carrots, cut sliced into rounds

2   bay leaves

4   cloves

4   juniper berries

4   tablespoons (50 g) brown sugar

1   cup (200 ml) red wine or cider vinegar

1   pinch of chili powder

    freshly ground pepper and peppercorns

    sunflower oil

DIRECTION

1. Arrange fillets in a shallow dish and cover them
    with milk.

2. Leave to desalinate for half an hour. Then take them out,
    rinse them under the tap, and dry on paper towels.

3. Boil the vinegar, the sugar, the cloves, the juniper, and
    the sliced carrots for a few minutes. Add a pinch of chili
    pepper. Add some oil.

4. Remove the carrots and some of the spices.

5. Arrange the fillets in a terrine. Layer lightly with the
    carrots, onions, bay leaves, and a little pepper.

6. Cover with the remaining vinegar, oil, and the extra
    spices. If the fillets are still dry, add oil until they
    are well coated.

7. Allow to cool and marinate in the refrigerator for two
    weeks before serving.

HERRING UNDER A FUR COAT

TANYA'S RECIPE

INGREDIENTS

1   whole herring in brine

2   large cooked beets

5   potatoes, steamed in advance, then peeled, then chilled

2   cooked carrots, also refrigerated

3   hard-boiled eggs

    a few cooked peas

1   bunch of chives or 2 young onions

1   cup of homemade mayonnaise lightened with yogurt

    parsley

DIRECTIONS

Cut the herring into cubes.

On different plates, grate the chilled and peeled potatoes, as well as the beets, onions, eggs, and carrots.

1. On a round or fish-shaped dish, place a layer of herring.

2. Cover the herring with finely chopped or finely sliced onions. Add a little sunflower oil to absorb the strong taste of onions.

3. Add the grated potatoes in one layer about half an inch thick, then cover with a very thin layer of mayonnaise.

4. Follow with another layer of herring pieces and a thin layer of mayonnaise.

5. Add a layer of grated, cooked carrots, cover with mayonnaise.

6. Now add a layer of grated hard-boiled eggs; cover with mayonnaise.

7. Add a layer of grated beets and finish with a last layer of mayonnaise, this time slightly thicker.

8. Decorate the top with the remaining eggs and/or the cooked peas. Sprinkle with parsley, dill, or chives.

9. Let cool for at least 30 minutes before serving with vodka.

HERRINGS IN CREAM SAUCE
POLISH STYLE

INGREDIENTS

2 packages (500 g) smoked herring fillets, approximately
6-8 fillets

4 onions

1 cup (250 ml) red-wine vinegar

3 tablespoons (35 g) sugar

2 tablespoons oil

4-5 tablespoons sour cream

6 peppercorns

DIRECTIONS

1. Peel and cut the onions into slices.

2. Plunge them into a pot with water, 2½ tablespoons sugar, $^7/_8$ cup vinegar, and simmer until the onions are tender.

3. Chop the herring into pieces, and marinate it for an hour in the remaining vinegar, sugar, pepper, and spices.

4. Collect the liquid from the herring in a bowl, and mix with the drained onions, cream, and oil to make a smooth sauce.

5. Add the herring to the sauce, mix, and let stand for two hours before serving.

BERLINER ROLLMOPS
IN REMOULADE

Ges.
gesch.

C.V.
M.

Handels-
marke

HERRINGS IN MUSTARD SAUCE

(SWEDISH RECIPE, FROM ANNA ANDREASSON, OF THE KLÄDESHOLMEN SEAFOOD COMPANY)

INGREDIENTS

2   cups (500 g) pickled herring fillets or rollmops, approximately 6-8 fillets

½   cup (100 ml) sweet mustard

½   cup (100 ml) Dijon mustard

1½ cups (150 ml) brown sugar

2   teaspoons white vinegar

½   (100 ml) cup vegetable oil

1   small bunch of dill, chopped

3   leeks, cut into small pieces (white parts only)

1-3 teaspoons of whiskey (or vodka, or aquavit, as desired) black pepper

DIRECTIONS

1. Cut the herring fillets diagonally into pieces, and drain them.

2. Add the leeks.

3. Mix the mustard, the sugar, and the vinegar in a bowl.

4. Add the oil, drop by drop, stirring well as you go.

5. Repeat process with the whiskey (or vodka).

6. Add pepper to taste.

7. Place the herrings in a terrine, add the sauce, making sure the herring is well coated.

8. Marinate in the refrigerator before serving.

POTATO SALAD WITH HERRING

GERMAN RECIPE

OPPOSITE The back of a matchbook displayed this advertisement for Vita, a famous American brand of canned fish-related products.

INGRÉDIENTS

2   jars pickled herring or rollmops, approximately 7-10 fillets

5½ cups (1 kg) Idaho potatoes

3   dill pickles, cut into slices

1   tablespoon capers

1   onion, freshly chopped

½   cup white wine

FOR THE SEASONING

1⅓ cup (200 g) sour cream or *crème fraîche*

1   teaspoon lemon juice

3   tablespoons white wine or cider vinegar

½   cup oil

1   tablespoon sugar

salt, pepper

few slices of radish or dill for decoration

DIRECTIONS

1. Steam the potatoes with their skins. When tepid, peel them, cut them into slices and place them in a bowl.

2. Warm the wine. Pour over the potatoes.

3. Add the pickles, the capers, the herring (cut into pieces), and the onion.

4. In a separate bowl, mix the lemon juice and *crème fraîche* (if you're using it) and let stand for 20 minutes.

5. In another bowl, combine the remaining ingredients of the seasoning, add the sour cream (or lemon and *crème fraîche* mixture), mix well and pour over other ingredients. Stir gently so as not to break up the potatoes.

6. Allow to cool in the refrigerator, then decorate before serving.

BIBLIOGRAPHY

Breukels, Guillaume, Jean-Joseph Raepsaet, Jacobus Baert
Note sur la découverte de caquer le hareng (1816)
Livre numérique Google.
Cros, Charles, *Le théâtre du hareng saur : Le monologue selon*
Charles Cros et Coquelin Cadet, anthologie de monologues
1880-1900, Éditions La Fontaine, 2009.
Deutsch, Jonathan, and Rachel D. Sachs, *Jewish American Food*
Culture, Bison Books, 2009.
Dumas, Alexandre, *Grand dictionnaire de la cuisine,*
Editions Pierre Grobel 1873.
Durand, Jacky, *Le hareng de nos mers,*
Les Quatre Chemins, 2009.
Ezgulian, Sonia, *Le hareng, dix façons de le préparer,*
Les Éditions de l'Épure, 2009.
Federman, Mark Russ, *Russ & Daughters,*
Schocken Books, 2013.
Fidler, Cathie, *Recettes à la vie, à l'amour,* Au Pays Rêvé
éditions, 2011.
Gautier, Alban, *Du hareng pour les princes, du hareng pour les*
pauvres, IXème – XIIIème siècles, Google
Huysmans, Jorris-Karl, *Le drageoir aux épices,*
G. Crès et Cie, 1921.
Laurioux, Bruno, *Manger au moyen âge,*
Hachette Littérature, 2002.
Lefevere, Sylvain, *Le hareng,* dans Les Carnets du Service
Éducatif, Institut Royal des Sciences Naturelles de Belgique.
Carnet n°9, 1960.
Rosten, Leo, *The Joys of Yiddish,* W. H. Allen Limited, 1968.
Grossinger, Jennie, *The Art of Jewish Cooking,*
Random House, 1958.
Roden, Claudia, *The Book of Jewish Food,*
Alfred A. Knopf, 1996.
Rozensztroch, Daniel *Hangers,* Editions Du Passage, 2002.
Rozensztroch, Daniel, and Shiri Slavin, *Brush,*
Pointed Leaf Press, 2005.
Slesin, Suzanne, and Stafford Cliff, Daniel Rozensztroch,
Mittel Europa, Clarkson N. Potter, 1994.
Slesin, Suzanne, and Stafford Cliff, Daniel Rozensztroch, Gilles
de Chabaneix, Jean-Louis Ménard, *Wire,* Abbeville Press, 1994.
Smylie, Mike, *Herring, A History of the Silver Darlings,*
The History Press, 2011.
Talila, *Mon Yiddish Blues,* Naïve, 2009.

WEBSITES
In French:
http://aquaculture-aquablog.blogspot.fr/2011/04/alaska-
hareng-tsunami-japon.html
http://www.thecanadianencyclopedia.com/articles/fr/hareng
http://www.lemonde.fr/voyage/article/2010/11/04/un-hareng-
peut-en-cacher-un-autre_1435595_3546.html
http://www.courrierinternational.com/article/2003/09/18/le-
hareng-un-plat-de-l-extreme
http://www.academia.edu/509176/Du_hareng_pour_les_

princes_du_hareng_pour_les_pauvres_IXe-XIIIe_siecle_)
http://www.carnets-de-traverse.com/blog/musee-du-hareng
http://www.lemonde.fr/voyage/article/2010/11/04/un-hareng-
peut-en-cacher-un-autre_1435595_3546.html
http://www.lexpress.fr/culture/livre/sur-le-hareng_809201.html
http://www.france-pittoresque.com/spip.php?article455
http://www.centrostudilaruna.it/symbolisme-et-signification-
des-poissons-dans-les-mythologies-indo-europeennes.html
http://pierre.painset.free.fr/menu4/hgs_97_1.htm
http://www.fecamp-terre-neuve.fr/Historique/Apercu3.html
http://www.confrerieduhareng.net/11.html
http://lartdesmets.e-monsite.com/pages/la-peche-au-moyen-
age/le-hareng-au-moyen-age.html
http://cepb.info/livre-sthareng.html
http://www.kitchenbazar.fr/article-le-jour-des-harengs-
forshmak-64191132.html
http://kitchenbazar.eu/
http://sante.lefigaro.fr/mieux-etre/nutrition-aliments/hareng/
quels-sont-ses-bienfaits
http://www.pitchipoi.com/herring.html
http://www.saveurs-npdc.com/produit_details.php?num=54
http://memoires1table.canalblog.com/
archives/2008/08/22/10272080.html
http://www.leguidedesconnaisseurs.be/
http://odysee-islandaise.over-blog.com/article-l-epopee-des-
harengs-38762008.html
http://www.visitsweden.com/suede/-voir-et-a-faire/
Swedish-Lifestyle/Saisons-et-traditions/Le-hareng-fermente-
Surstromming/
In English:
http://www.sliammonfirstnation.com/archaeology/
herringarch.html
http://thetyee.ca/News/2011/11/04/BC-Herring/
http://herringschool.wordpress.com/
http://www.thecanadianencyclopedia.com/articles/fr/hareng
http://www.pac.dfo-mpo.gc.ca/index-eng.html
http://www.herringpondtribe.com/
http://jhom.com/topics/salt/herring.htm
http://yiddishwit.com/
http://cassgidley.org/news-and-events/herring-festival/
http://antikbar.co.uk/
http://www.gtyarmouth.co.uk/Tooke-Books/html/gt_
yarmouth_herring_industry.htm
http://www.historyshelf.org/secf/silver/02.php
http://www.bbc.co.uk/nationonfilm/topics/fishing/
http://photos.shetland-museum.org.uk/index.php
http://www.thistleandbroom.com/scotland/herring-girls.htm
http://www.jewisheastend.com/index.html
http://www.bismarckhering.com/index-eng.php3
http://www.educationscotland.gov.uk/scotlandssongs/
secondary/songofthefishgutters.asp
In Swedish:
http://www.kajakrapporten.se/sillens-helg-i-bohuslan/

AUTHORS' NOTES

We took note of many other very important things when writing this book. For instance, that a driftnet is a net that is towed through the water, between the surface and the sea bed, without entering into contact with the latter. And then, that the Americans and the French had a meeting of minds in mid-Atlantic, calling that ocean, respectively, "The Herring Pond" and "La mer aux harengs"—this last term was used in the days when the French penal colony was at Cayenne and the convicts had to be transported across the Atlantic for their rest cure. Next came Alexandre Dumas, who revealed the secret of the "red herring" when, in his *Dictionary of Cuisine*, he wrote: "As late as the 16th century, there still survived a rather bizarre custom among the Canons of Rheims Cathedral. On Ash Wednesday, after the Tenebrae, they would move in procession to the church of Saint-Rémi, two abreast, each dragging behind him a herring on a string. Every one of the Canons tried hard to step on the herring of the man in front of him while trying to protect his own one from the man behind him. This extravagant custom came to an end only when the procession ceased to be."

Likewise, we learned that it was on the island of Marstrand that the first synagogue in Sweden was established, in the 1780s. The same Swedes claim it was they (not the Dutch) who invented the curing technique. Yet they forget all about that when they ferment herrings in cans, which custom, we hear, is banned by some airlines on the grounds that they could explode in mid-flight. But who are we to judge?

We thought we'd leave our readers with a few unresolved enigmas so that they can go fishing for more information on their own. They could, for example, follow the work of the multidisciplinary team set up in British Columbia under Dana Lepofski of the Simon Fraser University; this includes scientists and members of the First Nations, all working together to reconstruct the history and migrations of this wonderful fish.

On the other hand, you don't need to be very learned to know that for Sephardim, it's sardine heads that are supposed to make Jews (and other people) intelligent. And as for a sense of humor, why, that's one of those simple gifts that come free.

One last anecdote then, to conclude and illustrate what the French singer Talila, that graceful interpreter of the Yiddish song tradition, expresses so charmingly when she says: "Proust had his madeleine. *Our* madeleine is herring and onions."

My own German-born Jewish mother is now in her nineties, but she's still preparing herrings (with sour cream) every time my little brother comes to visit, for he's crazy about them.

Once, he came to visit to celebrate her ninety-third birthday in style. Now, here's a conversation between the two of us a few days before the great event. The herrings had been duly purchased and prepared, and were waiting in the refrigerator:

"Mom, do you remember that your darling son is coming this weekend?"

"Yes, that's right, he's arriving on Friday."

"And do you know what he's coming for?"

"Yes, of course I do…." A moment's hesitation, as her memory is not always quite what it was. But her reply couldn't have been clearer.

"To eat my herrings."

What else?

Natürlich!

Quoi d'autre?

Vos noch?

INDEX

DEDICATION

This book is dedicated to the memory of those, who while no longer with us, inspired us: Léon Giler, Marthe Kristeller, Margot Schertz, Sonia Fidler, and Sonia Rozensztroch.

ACKNOWLEDGMENTS

The authors thank Piotr Nezdeshny for his translation of the French text and the people and institutions that kindly agreed to contribute to their project: Anna Andreasson (Sweden); Christian Thévenin (France – Collections from the Musée de Sarreguemines); Dana Lepofski (Canada—Simon Fraser University); Grand Central Station Oyster Bar, NY – USA; Inka Petersen (Sausalito Herring Festival Poster); Iris Lippach (Germany – Musée de la Céramique Villeroy & Boch); Johanna Kovitz and www.Yiddishwit.com; Kirill Kalinin (AntikBar Original Vintage Posters); Mairie de Beaumont le Hareng (France); Russ & Daughters, New York, NY; Mairie et Office du Tourisme de Fécamp (France); Merci, Paris, France; Nederlands Visbureau (The Netherlands); Willemine Nataf (Consulate of the Netherlands, Nice, France).

On a more personal note, Daniel Rozensztroch and Cathie Fidler would also very much like to thank all those who, in different ways have helped, supported, and encouraged this adventure: Adrienne Dubessay; Alix Brijatoff; Anne-Marie Casès; Anne-Marie Foggin; Antoine Bootz; Catherine Ardoin; Catherine et Marcel Sabaton; Christine Puech; Edith Champseix; Fabienne Rousso-Lenoir; Florence Kahn; Francis Amiand; Françoise et Roland De Leu; Isabelle Reisinger; Jacotte Bobroff; Jacques Lefebvre-Linetzky; Jean-Luc Colonna d'Istria; Jean-Pierre Faugué; Jos Van de Ven; Marie-France Cohen; Michèle Merowka; Nathalie Hazan; Paola Navone; Peter Burnett; Servane Gaxotte; Shiri Slavin; Suzanne Czernichow; Suzanne Lind; Suzanne Tarica; Suzette et Guy Slama; Talila Guteville; Tanya Ilisavskaya; Valérie Solvi; William Aidan; and Niki Russ Federman of Russ & Daughters.

And, of course: At Pointed Leaf Press, publisher Suzanne Slesin, for her enthusiasm and support; creative director Frederico Farina who knew so well how to work with the ephemera and photographs of the terrines in the collection; as well as Kelly Koester and Marion D. S. Dreyfus.

THE AUTHORS

DANIEL ROZENSZTROCH has been a longtime consultant to the magazine *Marie-Claire Maison* and is now the creative director of the Merci shop in Paris, France. He is also the co-author of a series of titles in the Style Series published by Clarkson N. Potter, as well as a number of books on the subject of everyday things that include *Wire* and *Kitchen Ceramics* (Abbeville Press); *Glass* (Harry N. Abrams); *Hangers* (Editions Le Passage); and *Brush* (Pointed Leaf Press).

CATHIE FIDLER who lives in Nice, France, was a teacher of EFL for many years before publishing two novels (with Au Pays Rêvé éditions) and three collections of short stories, among which is *In Hazy Zones*, published in English (Edilivre éditions). She is particularly interested in history and in what has been passed down from one generation to the next. Some of the articles on her blog (http://gratitude-leblogdecathiefidler.blogspot.fr/) are posted in English.

CREDITS

CAPTIONS

COVER This German terrine from the 1930s bears an inscription in Gothic lettering and a checkerboard border that recalls kitchen tiles of the period.

ENDPAPERS We open and close this book—dedicated to ceramic items, most of them manufactured in Germany—with a couple of bills dating back to 1928. Both were sent from the German North Sea port of Emden. Many Dutch Protestants fleeing persecution settled there in the 17th century, thus contributing to the city's prosperity, abundance, culture, religion, tolerance, art and beauty. Such are the themes that our beloved fish has enabled us to delve into.

BACK OF FRONT ENDPAPERS AND PAGE 1 This unusual postcard consists of an illustration depicting a herring, and is accompanied by a postmarked Swedish stamp with an effigy of the same fish. Issued by the Fisheries Institute, it was part of a series intended to give maximum distribution to information about oceans and, in general, all matters that touched on life at sea.

PAGES 2-3 *A Morning Catch of Herring* says the caption of this card sent from Lowestoft, a fishing port on the east coast of England. The image gives an immediate idea of the quantity of herrings that could be caught in a single night.

PAGE 4 The 1635 *Still Life With Stag Beetle*, an oil painting, is by the German artist Georg Flegel (1566-1638), one of the first realist painters, and one of those most admired in 17th century Germany. The beetle is the star player, but the other elements represented, including the herring, give an idea of everyday life at the time.

PAGES 6-7 An advertisement for a brand of chicory—*Chicorée Paul Mairesse—Cambrai*—has the same design as was used by several other brands, especially makers of chocolate. It is interesting to note the small size of the herring boat.

PAGE 8 The French city of Fécamp, in Normandy, celebrates the herring in all its forms at an annual festival in November. They sell them, they grill them, and they eat them all along the waterfront. Visitors can admire the techniques of yesteryear during guided visits to the old fish processing factories.

PAGE 193 This tiny terrine was part of a china dollhouse set so little girls so could have tea parties for their dolls. The fact that an item like this should have been reproduced in miniature proves, once more, what an essential place soused herrings played in the everyday lives of so many German families.

ISBN:978-1-938461-21-7 Library of Congress Control Number: 2014936800 FIRST EDITION 10 9 8 7 6 5 4 3 2 1 PRINTED IN ITALY

Mariniertе Heringe

August Jasper & S

Telegr.-Adr.:
August Jasper - Emden.
Fernsprecher: Nr. 2067 u. 2366

Gegrü
Reichsbank–Giro–Konto
Postscheckkonto: Hannover

Faktura für

Herrn   Wilhelm Br

Firma

Erfüllungsort Emden für Lieferung und Zahlung.

A. J.

№   **1458**

Sie empfangen laut Ihrer Bestellung für I

1/1 Tp. Prima Emder Voll

Zahlbar spätestens

Sollte obiger Betrag bis dahin
so nehmen wir an, daß Sie
wir ihn per Post zuzügl.

[handschriftlich:] Besten Dank, mit freuden ... wieder das allerfeinste. Billigst ... ergebenst ...

Netto-Kasse oh